THE GERMAN AIR RAIDS
ON GREAT BRITAIN, 1914-1918

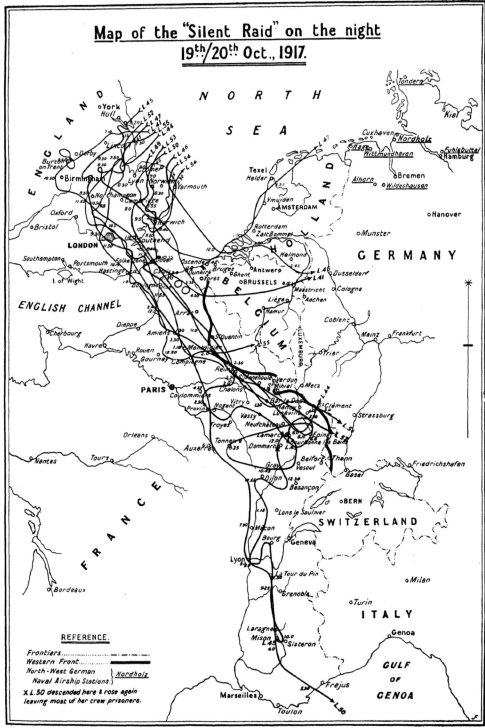

Map of the "Silent Raid" on the night 19ᵗʰ/20ᵗʰ Oct., 1917.

REFERENCE.

Frontiers ....
Western Front ....
North-West German
Naval Airship Stations.) _Nordholz_
X L.50 descended here & rose again
leaving most of her crew prisoners.

From an Official Report prepared by the War Office. Reproduced by permission of the Controller, H.M. Stationery Office.

On this occasion eleven German naval airships, which came from Tondern, Nordholz, Alhorn and Wittmundhaven, crossed the English coast between East Anglia and the East Riding. At the very great height—some four miles up—at which they were compelled to fly by the defences, they were caught in a gale of some sixty miles an hour, with the result that the fleet was forced south-eastwards through England and France. One ship was shot down near Nancy by the French; two others were forced to land in France; and another after an attempted landing was blown out to the Mediterranean. The remainder eventually got back, but one was wrecked to destruction on landing. When the main body drifted over London, quite unconsciously, the guns and searchlights were forbidden to open up so as not to disclose to the raiders their whereabouts. By a curious fluke a bomb dropped at random fell in Piccadilly. In view of the negative action of the London defences this raid became known as the "Silent Raid."

The German Air Raids on Great Britain, 1914-1918. Captain Joseph Morris. Sampson Low.

THE
GERMAN AIR RAIDS
ON GREAT BRITAIN

1914-1918

BY

CAPTAIN JOSEPH MORRIS

B.A. (CANTAB.), A.F.R.Ae.S. (LATE R.A.F.)

The Naval and Military Press

This edition of

THE GERMAN AIR RAIDS ON GREAT BRITAIN
1914-1918

first published 1993 by

THE NAVAL & MILITARY PRESS,
DALLINGTON,
EAST SUSSEX

Publishing History

First published *c*.1925 by Sampson Low, Marston
& Co. Ltd..

This edition is now reproduced exactly as the original
volume, complete and unabridged.

New material and binding design by

LANGLANDS EDITION
Loughborough

PREFACE

DURING the war nearly 9,000 German bombs of a total weight of some 280 tons were dropped on British soil in the course of fifty-one airship and fifty-two aeroplane attacks. London was bombarded twelve times by airship and nineteen times by aeroplane. In all 1,413 persons were killed and 3,408 others were wounded as the result of these raids, London suffering more than half of the casualties—670 killed and 1,962 injured. The underlying motive of these raids was to unnerve the British public, to make life unbearable by destroying their homes and by crippling their means of supply; and, by inflicting heavy casualties, to compel them to sacrifice their national honour rather than suffer a continuance of air attacks. In this the Germans failed.

An attempt is here made to tell for the first time the story of this menace—how it was started, how it grew and how it was countered. Only the most authentic sources of information have been drawn upon. By the courtesy of the Air Ministry I was given access to official records and in particular to an excellent series of Air Raid Reports which were drawn up during the war by the War Office concurrently with the raids. I have also consulted *The War in the Air*, Volume I, by the late Sir Walter Raleigh, the official air historian; *Naval Operations*, Volumes II and III, by the late Sir Julian Corbett, the official naval historian; and the articles in the *Encyclopædia Britannica—Air Raids*, by Major General E. B. Ashmore, and *Air Defence*, by Colonel M. St. L. Simon. On the German side I have made use of the official naval history *Der Krieg Zur See*, 1914–1918, *Nord See*, Volumes III and IV, by Korvettenkapitan O. Groos; Neumann's *The German Air Force in the Great War;* and an informative article by Lieutenant von Schiller in the *Marine Rundschau* for March–April, 1922, *The Development and Objects of the German Naval Airship Service*.

The heroes of this book are the gallant airmen who went up into the void to assert the inviolability of British air. All who died on this heroic service in conflict with the enemy are here remembered. The deeds of many of those who fortunately are still with us are here also remembered, but where gallant deeds are as numerous as the motes which people a sunbeam I have had great difficulty in the selection. Many perforce were unrecorded and several may have escaped my notice, so that the few given can only be regarded as representative of the whole. Perhaps in no service was a greater uniform level maintained than in the Air Force, and it is to this the British air service largely owes its pre-eminence.

I am also indebted to the War Office, the Air Ministry, and the Controller of His Majesty's Stationery Office for permission to use maps from which those here given have been made, also for permission to reproduce photographs. I am under a similar obligation to the Imperial War Museum and the Royal Aeronautical Society.

I have taken great care to ensure accuracy, but where one has to act as judge and jury as well as counsel for the prosecution and for the defence, and where moreover the evidence is frequently slender and conflicting, and witnesses are unavailable, it is inevitable that mistakes will be made.

I should like to acknowledge the kindly help and unfailing courtesy which I have received at the hands of the staff of the Historical Branch of the Air Ministry.

JOSEPH MORRIS.

Sloane Court,
London, S.W.3.

CONTENTS

PART ONE

THE AIRSHIPS

ix

CONTENTS

PART TWO

THE AEROPLANES

LIST OF ILLUSTRATIONS

xi

LIST OF MAPS

PART ONE

THE GERMAN AIR RAIDS ON GREAT BRITAIN, 1914-1918

PART ONE

THE AIRSHIPS

CHAPTER I

THE BRITISH NAVY STRIKES WHILE GERMANY PREPARES

On the outbreak of the Great War in 1914 the air forces of the various nations involved were so small and of such recent development that the uses to which aircraft might be put, other than gaining intelligence, were only vaguely conceived. It is not surprising, therefore, that such conventions as had been drawn up with regard to the use of aircraft in war were as scanty as they were indefinite. Even with regard to peaceful uses, international jurists indulged in lofty rhetoric and drew up monumental documents to decide the nationality of a child born while on board an aircraft.

At the Hague conference in 1899 a vote was passed prohibiting aircraft from discharging projectiles or explosives, but they were left free to be used for intelligence and other purposes. This prohibition was accepted by all the Powers and was to be in force for five years. During these five years, however, aviation had made great progress. The first Zeppelin was completed and flown in 1900, and in 1903 the Wright brothers had carried out the first free flight in a power-driven aeroplane. The significance of these events was reflected in the Hague conference of 1907. Clauses relating to aircraft were so vague and ambiguous as to render them nugatory and, further, they were not accepted by many of the principal Powers. So that for all practical purposes it was recognised that expediency and expediency alone would decide the uses to which aircraft would be put in war and limitations would be material or moral, according to the temper of the belligerent.

That in the event of war Germany would use her airships to deliver attacks on Great Britain there was no doubt. As to the means of dealing with the menace expert opinion was both divided and oscillatory. To those who favoured the airship itself as the counter weapon the *Mayfly* disaster of 1911 was a severe blow. This rigid airship had been built, firstly, to gain experience of the capabilities of such craft, and secondly for naval reconnaissance. At the time of the formation of the Royal Flying Corps, in May, 1912, the position was desperate. No British gun had as yet been made which could be relied on to hit an airship; so that vulnerable points, whilst being fully exposed to aerial attack, had no means of defence whatsoever.

British Naval Rigid Airship No. 1—The *Mayfly*—at Cavendish Dock, Barrow,
September, 1911

The wreck of the *Mayfly*, 24th September, 1911

To face p. 4

The remarkable performances of the *Schwaben*, the *Siemens-Schukert* and the latest *Parseval* airships in Germany, forced the menace again into prominence. Stories of ghost-like airships hovering in the North Sea began to gain ground and action could no longer be delayed. The army undertook to provide quick-firing guns both fixed and mobile and the navy concentrated on semi-automatics capable of being used in light cruisers and destroyers. Both these guns were expressly intended for dealing with airships. Progress with them was slow; and owing to pressure by the Admiralty the War Office, as a temporary measure, mounted 6-inch howitzers, two apiece, at the Chattenden and Lodge Hill magazines. In April, 1913, it was stated that these guns were " in a position to open fire without delay." In the meantime orders had been given for the quick-firing guns, but deliveries did not take place until a few months before the outbreak of war.

The navy and army each had clearly defined duties and spheres of operation in the event of war. But the air service presented difficulties which were by no means easy of solution. The air is common to land and sea and aircraft can fly over both. Aircraft can observe for the fleet or for the army and the same aircraft can attack a battleship or a military objective. The counter measures in so far as aircraft versus aircraft are concerned are the same. So that with two virtually separate air forces the problem of aerial defence was considerably complicated. Broadly, the War Office claimed the sole responsibility not only in regard to everything inland but in regard to naval ports and vulnerable points of all kinds, even those exclusively of naval interest. The navy were to confine themselves to the protection of the coast.

These paper arrangements were not passively accepted by the Admiralty. To facilitate the co-operation of the naval air service with the fleet, they decided at the outset that naval air stations were to be situated at points along the coast ranging from Calshot in the south to Scapa Flow in the Orkneys. This disposition of the naval air stations was most favourable for dealing with hostile air attacks in the event of war and this aspect formed an important item in naval air policy. But the navy had never trusted to the defensive. They considered that whilst passive measures were useful as safeguards, the real key to the situation would be found to lie in a vigorous and offensive attack on the enemy's airsheds, etc., and on his aircraft before they reach these shores.

The Royal Flying Corps had not, up to the declaration of war, been provided with aeroplanes for home defence. They had been limited as a matter of prior urgency to the development of expeditionary squadrons, and on the outbreak of war practically all their serviceable aeroplanes were taken abroad by the four squadrons which had been mobilised. Not only were none available for guarding vulnerable points, but few could be found even for the temporary purpose of coast-watching during the passage of the army to the Continent. When the decision was arrived at that the whole of the eastern coast of the British Isles was to be patrolled by aircraft, Sir David Henderson, the Director-General of Military Aeronautics, represented that, as far as the Military Wing was concerned, the few pilots and mechanics available would be best employed for training. In the event, the Admiralty undertook the task of patrolling the east coast of England, including the Tyne and the Humber, and the War Office was made responsible for the Scottish coast and the south-east coast of England, including the Thames estuary and the Channel. In addition the navy provided aerial patrols to watch the safe passage of the Expeditionary Force to France.

The Royal Naval Air Service, on the other hand, were not in a position to co-operate with the fleet, as the advance in seaplanes had been slow and no suitable airships had been provided. They had a large number of aeroplanes available and so before the war was a month old Lord Kitchener, realising the impossibility of the War Office carrying out their technical responsibility for home defence against air attack was only too glad to hand over the responsibility to the Admiralty and the First Lord Mr. Churchill readily undertook it. The handing over took place on the 3rd of September, 1914. But the navy had already taken independent steps. The air unit under

Commander C. R. Samson, which had been sent to Ostend on the 27th of August, to assist the marine brigade, was shortly afterwards withdrawn to Dunkirk with a view of returning to England. But on the 1st of September the force was ordered to remain there to " deny the use of territory within a hundred miles of Dunkirk to German Zeppelins and to attack by aeroplanes all airships replenishing there." Thus began the offensive co-operation of the naval air service in home defence which almost up to the end of the war was to be most efficacious in preventing air attacks on this country.

Nominally the Dunkirk force consisted of three squadrons of twelve machines each, together with some sixty armed motor cars, but actually it fell far short of this establishment. On the 3rd September, Squadron Commander E. L. Gerrard arrived at Ostend with three additional machines for the purpose of raiding Dusseldorf and Cologne. Unfortunately, whilst he was away in Antwerp looking for a suitable aerodrome, on the 12th a very heavy gale blew up and wrecked the machines which had perforce been pegged out in the open. Other machines were got ready and a base for the attack was formed at Antwerp. On the 22nd September, two machines set out to attack Dusseldorf and two Cologne. Owing to thick mist only one pilot Flight Lieutenant C. H. Collet, reached his objective. He came down to 400 feet and bombed the airship shed at Dusseldorf, but with no success. The second attempt was more fruitful. On the 8th October, Flight Lieutenant R. L. G. Marix flew to Dusseldorf and completely destroyed an airship shed there, together with an airship housed in it. Squadron Commander D. A. Spenser Grey was not so successful at Cologne owing to heavy mist, so he discharged his missiles on the main railway station. The evacuation of Antwerp on this very day put a stop to these activities for a time.

The next blow was masterly in conception and superb in execution. Four new Avros straight from Manchester were secretly and swiftly taken to Belfort, and on the 21st November, Squadron Commander E. F. Briggs, Flight Commander J. T. Babington, Flight Lieutenant S. V. Sippe and Flight Sub-Lieutenant R. P. Cannon got ready for a flight to Friedrichshafen. Cannon damaged his machine in trying to leave the ground; the others got off well and made a bee line for their objective, which they all reached. They all dropped their bombs on the sheds and caused severe damage to a Zeppelin. Sippe and Babington got back safely but Briggs was shot down and taken prisoner. When the length of this flight—250 miles, the fact that it was over enemy territory, and the small power of the Avro are taken into account, this achievement easily ranks with the best of the war.

When on Christmas Day in 1914 the fleet made a demonstration in the Heligoland Bight with a view to inducing the German High Seas Fleet to come to action, seaplanes played their part. Their orders were to attack the airship sheds at Cuxhaven, or alternatively ships or military works. They failed to locate the sheds, but their mission was not entirely unsuccessful as they gleaned valuable information concerning the disposition of the German fleet.

Meanwhile, what of the Germans? In the German official naval history, Groos informs us that:

" As early as the end of September the Naval Staff and the Imperial Naval Board had jointly discussed the question as to whether airships should be used against England. On account of the small number of airships available and in view of their great importance for fleet reconnaissance work, it appeared advisable to wait to use them for raids until there was big enough reserve for both purposes. At the end of October the employment of airships, which was urged by the Command at the front, was again prohibited. When the requisite number was reached at the end of December, other difficulties stood in the way. It was first intended that the whole of the aerial forces should make an attack in co-operation with the army; the army, however, wished first of all to use its Z airships to attack the French fortified towns of Nancy, Dunkirk and Verdun. Matters were further complicated by the fact that the Imperial Chancellor was anxious that London should not be included amongst the places raided in England. The Chief of the Naval Staff,

An Avro Aeroplane of the type used for the raid on the German airship sheds at Friedrichshafen on the 21st November, 1914

To face p. 10

however, held the view that London, with its important military establishments on the lower Thames was a highly important target, if airships, in view of their extreme vulnerability and the anti-aircraft defences which might be expected to exist, were to be kept for attacking places where really decisive results might be expected. Further postponement would mean that the most suitable time of the year would be over and, moreover, there was always a chance that a repetition of the British air raid on December 25th would mean the destruction of the airships in their sheds before they had time to take part in any action." He quotes a memorandum on the policy of raiding London in which the Chief of the Naval Staff wrote: " I hold the view that we should leave no means untried to crush England and that successful air raids on London, in view of the already existing nervousness of the people, would prove a valuable means to this end."

Groos tells us that permission was given for the proposed airship raids on England on the 9th January, 1915, and that the Kaiser decided that these raids were to be

" expressly restricted to military shipyards, arsenals, docks, and in general, military establishments, and that London itself was not to be bombed." [1]

[1] *Der Krieg Zur See*, 1914–1918. Vol. iii, p. 182.

Whatever may have been her intentions, Germany had not on the outbreak of the war sufficient resources for carrying out any operations over England. The German navy possessed one solitary airship, the L.3. Even this had no definite base, that at Nordholz being established as an emergency measure on the outbreak of war. The German army, on the other hand, had some twenty airships, including eight Zeppelins and one Schutte Lanz, with numerous sheds to house them. This fleet, however, was severely crippled by a series of disasters. Z.V crashed in Poland, Z.VI at Cologne, Z.VII in the Argonne and Z.VIII at Badonvillers, all in August, 1914. In addition there were the two destroyed in their sheds at Dusseldorf and Friedrichshafen. Further, five new Zeppelins and two Schutte Lanz ships were appropriated by the navy, ostensibly for oversea reconnaissance.

The army airship service was thus at a low ebb, while the naval gained strength and importance. It is not surprising, therefore, that no airship attacks were delivered on England in 1914 and that the initiative should have passed entirely into the hands of the German navy. Even at the beginning of 1915, when the naval ships were ready, the weather was so unfavourable that the first attack had to be delayed until 19th January.

This enforced interval was made full use of in developing defensive measures in England. The gun defences at the time of the Admiralty taking over the responsibility were limited to thirty-three, of which three one-pounder pom-poms, were for the inner defence of London; the Admiralty, the Foreign Office and the Crown Agents each had one apiece. Woolwich arsenal had two pom-poms and the other twenty-eight guns, consisting of 3-inch and 4-inch quick-firers and one-pounder pom-poms, were mounted at vunerable points, mainly of naval importance. New guns and searchlights were hastily procured and mounted.

When difficulty was experienced in finding crews to man the searchlights, Sir Edward Henry, Chief Commissioner of the Metropolitan Police, stepped into the breach and provided 120 Special Constables, all willing volunteers. Again, when it was decided to regularise this force the Office of Works employees who were engaged in erecting the necessary platforms freely enlisted, and leavened with chief petty officers and pensioned naval gunlayers the Anti-Aircraft Corps of the Royal Naval Volunteer Reserve sprang into existence.

Measures were concerted for the co-ordination between the naval and military air services. The primary duty of army aeroplanes was to give assistance to the field army in opposing an enemy landing on the shores of Britain. Any aeroplane not required for this purpose was to act in conjunction with the naval air service in anti-aircraft defence. The Admiralty were to be solely responsible for the aerial protection of London and for the time being military aeroplanes to be stationed at Hounslow and Joyce Green were to assist until naval squadrons had sufficiently developed. The Admiralty were to provide aircraft for the defence of ports and for the attack of aircraft which had passed the coastline, but the War Office were to assist whenever possible. Anti-aircraft guns for London and other large cities were to be manned by the navy, while those for defended ports and vulnerable points were to be in the hands of the army. Flights were carried out to test the visibility of London by night and orders for restricted lighting were introduced.

London came to be dimmed on the 1st October, and the police up to a sixty mile radius were instructed to warn the city on the approach of hostile aircraft. Towards the end of the year the area of the London anti-aircraft defences was extended to a circle of six miles radius with Charing Cross as the centre, and the armament for its protection had been increased to two 3-inch 20 cwt., four six-pounders, six one-pounder pom-poms, twelve searchlights, and a volunteer corps of some thousand strong to serve them.

The expected raids were now imminent and five look-out posts were established on the east and south-east coasts between Folkestone and Shoe-buryness. There had been alarms. At the beginning of September many circumstantial reports were received to the effect that a hostile airship was harbouring in the hills of Cumberland and Westmorland and patrolling by night. Second Lieutenant B. C. Hucks was despatched on a Bleriot to reconnoitre the area with a view to finding the ship's anchorage, and soon established the fact that the reports were quite unreliable. In searchlight practice illuminated banks of cloud would suggest hosts of hovering Zeppelins. The public's nerves were on edge, but as night after night passed without confirming their fears they were lulled into a sense of security which was soon to be rudely shaken.

CHAPTER II

THE CAMPAIGN STARTS

ALTHOUGH the airship was recognised as the more formidable menace and as the most potent means of reaching England, the Germans showed impatience as the airship campaign was perforce longer and longer delayed, and turned to heavier-than-aircraft to break the lull before the oncoming storm. At about 1 p.m. on the 21st December a hostile machine appeared off Dover, dropped two bombs in the sea near the Admiralty pier and made off again. Three days later a morning visit was paid by an aeroplane which dropped at Dover the first bomb to fall on British soil. An aeroplane sent up failed to see it. A third attempt was made on Christmas Day. At 12.35 p.m. an Albatros seaplane appeared at Sheerness from the sea. It made up the mouth of the Thames and actually reached Erith, on the outskirts of London. In spite of the heavy anti-aircraft gunfire and the fact that six machines, three naval and three military, went up to engage it, it retraced its path and got away.

Meanwhile the German naval airship service emerged from the curtain of invisibility and entered the domain of observation. They had gained some experience in reconnaissance, pushed close up to the English coast, and had been in action against British warships during the demonstration off Heligoland on Christmas Day. Nordholz, which had early been chosen as the base, was now ready. A revolving double shed had been constructed to enable the airships to take the air from whatever point of the compass the wind blew. Nordholz was situated near Cuxhaven on the coastline between the Elbe and the Weser. At Fuhlsbuttel on the Elbe just north of Hamburg was situated a double shed belonging to the Hamburger Luftschiffhafen Gesellschaft, and this was appropriated by the navy for an airship base. It was from these sheds, Nordholz and Fuhlsbuttel, that the naval airship campaign on England was launched. Korvetten-kapitan Peter Strasser, the commander of the German naval airship service, had perfected his weapon and was now ready.

On the morning of 19th January, 1915, the shed doors at Nordholz and Fuhlsbuttel were opened and handling parties stood by to nurse three airships into the air. The vessels had been carefully ballasted in their sheds so that their buoyancy just exceeded their weight. L.3 and L.4 at Fuhlsbuttel and L.6 at Nordholz were ready for the great adventure and were cheered as they gracefully sailed into the air. Their objective was England. L.6, commanded by Oberleutnant Freiherr von Buttlar, when half way over, was compelled to return with failing engines. The L.3 (Kapitanleutnant Fritz) and the L.4. (Kapitanleutnant Graf von Platen) made Norfolk after passing over the Happisburgh light. They were not too well served by their meteorological office. They had taken note of the barometer, but they were not to know that on nearing England they would be met by rain and snow squalls and banks of fog. The L.3 entered at Ingham and about 8.30 p.m. flew over Yarmouth, where seven out of nine bombs dropped killed two persons and injured three, besides wrecking several small houses. The L.4 encircling the north-eastern portion of Norfolk, dropped odd bombs at various coastal towns and villages until she reached King's Lynn, the lights of which attracted von Platen's attention. He appears to have thought that he was near the mouth of the Humber, so on King's Lynn he unloaded seven of his nine high explosive bombs and the last of his seven incendiaries. A man and a woman were killed and thirteen persons were injured. He reported that his airship was heavily attacked by anti-aircraft guns and was followed by searchlights. Says Groos

" by thus opening hostilities the place in question had itself to thank that the airship defended herself by dropping seven 50 kg. H.E. bombs." [1]

[1] *Der Krieg Zur See*, 1914-1918. Vol. iii, p. 184.

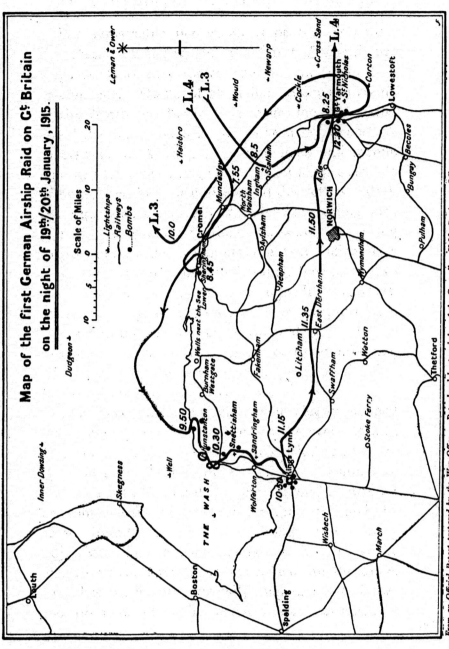

Map of the first German Airship Raid on Gt Britain on the night of 19th/20th January, 1915.

Scale of Miles

From an Official Report prepared by the War Office. Reproduced by permission of the Controller, H.M. Stationery Office.

This map shows the paths of the two Zeppelins which carried out the first German airship raid on Great Britain. The L.3, commanded by Kapitänleutnant Fritz, bombed Yarmouth, while the L.4, commanded by Kapitänleutnant Graf von Platen, bombed King's Lynn amongst other places. In all twenty-five bombs were dropped. At Yarmouth two people were killed and three others injured. At King's Lynn the casualties were two people killed and thirteen others injured.

The German Air Raids on Great Britain, 1914-1918.   Captain Joseph Morris.   Sampson Low.

The anti-aircraft guns existed only in von Platen's imagination and the searchlights were none other than the glare in the southern fog of the lights of Lynn.

So far as the Germans were concerned the pioneer raid had been far from disappointing. Two Zeppelins had bombed East Anglia and returned unscathed. The British public were less alarmed than indignant. They were not content with the passive measures of more and more darkening. They urged that active means must be devised for bringing the raiders to action. But they did not understand the immensity of the problem. They did not know that in spite of the size of a Zeppelin it was not easy to see it in a haze either from the ground or in the air, and further, that it did not present much of a target to the few and crude anti-aircraft guns available. To deal with airships which evaded fixed guns—as did the L.3 and L.4 —mobile defence was quickly improvised by the anti-aircraft corps. Machine-guns with high-angle mountings were installed on motor-chassis together with searchlights. With headquarters at Newmarket the eastern mobile section had for its field of action the whole of East Anglia. A southern section which was formed a fortnight later with headquarters at Caterham, only had a short existence.

If this inaugural effort was meant to be the first of a series, shortage of airships and the forces of nature combined to put a brake on the campaign

c

and the respite gave us three valuable months in which to put our defences in order. On the 17th February the raiders of Yarmouth and Lynn were caught in a snowstorm off the Jutland coast and were completely wrecked. On the 5th March the L.8 was blown back by a North Sea gale while attempting a raid on England, and fell a victim to the Nieuport batteries. She dropped amongst some trees at Tirlemont and there found her grave. She was, however, replaced three days later by the newly delivered L.9. Military airships of new and improved types were coming forward to make good the almost complete loss of the fleet which the army possessed on the outbreak of war. In peace time military airship sheds had been built throughout the length and breadth of the German Empire. But with Belgium in their hands the Germans were provided with the most convenient jumping-off ground for their air attacks on England. The first battle of Ypres had hardly died down before they began to establish airship bases at Gontrode, Evere, Berchem St. Agathe, and Etterbeek. Indeed, airships on reconnaissance to the Downs and off the coast at Cromer on the 22nd January, 1915, were believed to have started from one of these sheds. On the delivery of the new L.Z. spring models in the early part of 1915, they were concentrated in Belgium preparatory to being used against England, but while preparations were going forward the naval airship service still held the bâton.

In the early afternoon of the 14th April, L.9, commanded by Kapitanleutnant Mathy, was on a naval reconnaissance towards the coast of England. She was to return to her base before dark, but when within a hundred miles of Flamborough Head, Mathy, who had a good supply of bombs on board, decided to raid the Tyne, and by means of his wireless he obtained official sanction for the deed. The L.9 appeared off the mouth of the Tyne about 7 p.m. and coasted northwards to Blyth, before coming inland to swoop down on Tyneside. She was met by the rifle-fire of the 1st Battalion Northern Cyclists at Cambois. Mathy's first bomb fell in a field at West Sleekburn. This bomb was followed by twenty-two others before the Tyne was reached at about 8.40 p.m. He then unloaded his eight remaining bombs and went out to sea south of South Shields. The only casualties occurred at Wallsend, a woman and a child being injured. Two aeroplanes from Cramlington searched the skies for the L.9 in vain.

The next attack was carried out the following night by three ships, L.5 (Kapitanleutnant Böcker), L.6 (Oberleutnant Freiherr von Buttlar), and L.7 (Oberleutnant Peterson). The attack, led by Strasser himself on board the L.7, was intended for the Humber, but actually took place along the east coast, ranging from the Burnham flats in the north to the mouth of the Blackwater in the south. Groos' account of this raid is somewhat at variance with what we observed. L.7 is stated to have turned back when forty nautical miles south-east of the mouth of the Humber. He says:

"Scarcely had the airship turned eastward than she was violently attacked from ships beneath by automatic guns and machine-guns and had to seek safety at an altitude above 1,700 metres. Before reaching this altitude the airship was hit once forward and four times in the after portion."[1]

An airship which was made out by us to be the L.7 crossed the Norfolk coast at Burnham flats, flew along the coast east to Cromer and then followed the bend to Yarmouth where she went out to sea. She dropped no bombs on land and was unmolested either by guns or aeroplanes or as far as can be traced by warships.

Buttlar in the L.6 also reported being hit several times, soon after crossing the coast at the Naze, in addition to being caught in searchlight beams. As no searchlights were used at all throughout the raid and as the only three pom-pom shells fired returned to explode on the ground, the official German statement that:

"When the airship was berthed in the shed she was found to have two large and six smaller holes

[1] *Der Krieg Zur See*, 1914-1918. Vol. iv, p. 86.

from 2 to 10 centimetres in diameter made by
gunfire and 17 machine-gun hits,"[1]

is a tribute to the accuracy of the rifle-fire from
Landguard with the airship at 5,000 feet. Four
high explosive and thirty incendiary bombs were
dropped by Buttlar. They fell at Maldon and
Heybridge and injured a girl and damaged a house.

It fell to L.5, the spearhead of the attack, to drop
practically all the bombs. Henham Hall, Southwold,
and Lowestoft received the full force of the onslaught,
without, however, suffering any casualties. Flight
Commander de C. W. P. Ireland had risen in a
seaplane from Yarmouth shortly before one in the
morning; although he was in the air for three quarters
of an hour and near at hand he saw nothing of
Böcker. Like his comrades, Böcker reported the
ubiquitous guns and searchlights, although his
assailants were really the 6th Battalion Sussex
Cyclists at Easton Bavents. Had we but known
how frequently the raiders received hits we should
have felt less insecure with our slender defences in
those early days.

After the airship bases in Belgium had been
established, the military Zeppelins were tried out
by nocturnal excursions over the lines. Reports
of their presence were frequently coming to hand
and pilots would go up in an attempt to engage
them, but almost invariably failed to see them.

[1] *Der Krieg Zur See*, 1914–1918. Vol. iv, p. 87.

The Royal Flying Corps were not content with this state of affairs. With the object of reconnoitring the sheds, with a view to gaining information as to the best means of destroying them, Lieutenant L. G. Hawker started out on a B.E.2c on the 18th April, 1915. A clear afternoon was chosen to enable him the better to execute his mission. He carried three bombs which he was to drop over the Gontrode airship shed in order to test its defences. Hawker arrived over the shed at a height of about 6,000 feet and released two of his bombs. Above the shed was a large captive balloon and after the fall of his bombs sudden bursts of machine-gun fire appeared to come from the balloon. Hawker then shut down his engine and came down in a side-slipping spiral round and round the balloon, and by this means disconcerted the aim of the anti-aircraft gunners on the ground. He demoralised the machine-gunner in the balloon by throwing hand grenades on his downward journey. He reached within 200 feet of the ground and passing directly over the shed released his last bomb. He got away, but not before his machine had been hit by twenty-four bullets. This is one of the numerous gallant deeds of Hawker's distinguished career. A Zeppelin was reported the same night off the Sunk lightship, but the coast was not crossed and no raid materialised.

A few months later the persistent and successful offensive of the Royal Naval Air Service against these Belgian sheds made them so untenable that they were abandoned as permanent bases and were only used as emergency landing grounds. But this was not thought of when the German military air service light-heartedly launched its spring airship offensive on Great Britain. The first army raid was carried out by a solitary ship on the beautiful moonlight night of the 29th April, 1915. At 11.55 p.m. an airship crossed the coast at Old Felixstowe and went straight inland, reaching Ipswich shortly after midnight. After dropping a few bombs she continued in a straight line to Bury St. Edmunds, which she profusely peppered with bombs, many incendiary. After a double turn she went out on a course slightly north of her inward path, finally leaving the coast at Aldeburgh. The east coast was shrouded in fog. The objective may have been Stowmarket, where the explosive works, established before the war, were well known to the Germans. The airship commander, however, appears to have missed his objective owing to the fog, and when he came over a lighted town, he at once threw his bombs and made full speed back into the cover of the fog. In all, ten high explosive and sixty-six incendiary bombs were dropped. Casualties were nil, damage slight, and of action by guns or aeroplanes there was none.

Then followed three army raids on the Thames estuary as a prelude to the first raid on London.

On the 10th May, 1915, at 2.45 a.m. Hauptmann Linnarz on the L.Z.38 appeared over the prisoners of war hulk *Royal Edward*, moored off Southend, and dropped an incendiary close to the port side of the ship, flames leaping up to a height of some ten feet. Linnarz passed inland, but hastily turned about when over Canvey Island on being hit by the guns at Cliffe. He unloaded his bombs on Southend and went quickly out to sea by way of the Crouch. Although eleven machines ascended to attack him he was unobserved.

Linnarz left a card inscribed " You English. We have come and will come again. Kill or cure. German." He made good his boast.

Linnarz's next visit was to Thanet on the 17th May. He bombed Ramsgate and Oxney about two o'clock in the morning, but did not penetrate inland. He was fired on by the guardship in the Downs at 2.50 a.m., loitered in the neighbourhood of the North Goodwins till 3.25 a.m., and then went back to Belgium with the dawn of day, passing over the British lines at Armentieres. Flight Sub-Lieutenant R. H. Mulock, who had risen from Westgate in an Avro, caught Linnarz at a height of about 2,000 feet. Mulock at once opened fire, but his gun jammed, and before he could clear it the airship had passed out of view. Never again would Linnarz expose himself at such low levels. He was lucky to get away. On the same night Calais was bombed by the L.Z.37, and a third airship, the L.Z.39, was apparently out but did not raid. While L.Z.38 was being sought by aeroplanes and seaplanes which had risen from Westgate and Dover, the L.Z.39 passed Dunkirk at 3.15 a.m., going slowly eastwards, and all available machines there went up in pursuit. At 3.30 a.m. she was attacked off Nieuport by eight machines, three of which were able to get to close range. Flight Sub-Lieutenant R. A. J. Warneford, in a Nieuport with Leading Mechanic G. E. Meddis, observer, closed to attack, but the airship quickly climbed and got out of his reach. Flight Commander A. W. Bigsworth in an Avro, at a height of 10,000 feet, overtook the airship off Ostend. Passing over her from stern to bow he dropped four 20-lb. bombs fair along her back. Owing to heavy gunfire from the shore he broke off the combat and went out to sea. Just before Bigsworth's attack, Squadron Commander Spenser Grey, in a Nieuport, got into position some 50 to 100 feet below the ship and attacked her with machine-gun fire. When last seen the airship was proceeding to Ghent with her tail down.

It was common for the early raiders to report being caught in searchlight beams, but our records show Linnarz's was the first German airship over England to be thus fully illuminated in the early morning of the 17th May. To mark the historic occasion, the crew of the searchlight concerned were presented with a replica of the Anti-Aircraft Corps badge in silver.

On the 26th May, Linnarz paid his second visit to Southend. This was clearly a repetition of his earlier reconnaissance of the route to London, special attention being paid to the mouth of the Blackwater. At 10.30 p.m. the L.Z.38 appeared off Clacton-on-Sea. She then passed south-west via Badwell-juxta-Mare to Southminster. Here she was fired on by a pom-pom, and turned south to Burnham-on-Crouch shortly before 11 p.m. She passed over Shoeburyness under fire from a 3-inch anti-aircraft gun, and turned west to Southend, where she dropped twenty-three small high explosive bombs, or rather grenades, and forty-seven incendiary bombs. Three people were killed, and three were injured. The airship went off north-west, and was again engaged by Shoeburyness at 11.20 p.m. She passed Wakering and then proceeded via Burnham, where she was fired at by a company of the 2nd/8th Battalion Essex Regiment, thence to Badwell and out to sea at the mouth of the Blackwater shortly before midnight. Five naval aeroplanes went up from Eastchurch and Grain, but returned without having seen her; two were damaged on landing.

London was now clearly within reach, and when Sir Edward Henry called attention to the inadequacy of the preparations yet made for repelling attack, he was told that guns were on order. But none of these was ready, and some days later, when London had actually been raided, nothing more could be added to her defences than three guns diverted from the fleet. Apparently the Kaiser's embargo on raiding London was only in force as long as the objective was out of reach. As soon as it came within the range of practical politics, both von Bachmann, the Chief of Naval Staff, and von Falken-hayn, the Chief of the General Staff, pressed for a free hand. They were not content with territory east of the Tower. They represented that the most important objectives were not situated in that area.

They held that it would be a mistake to spare London, as this would not be understood by the German nation and would be regarded by the British as mere weakness. According to Groos, the Kaiser finally gave official permission for raids to be carried out on the city on the 20th July, the only restriction being that buildings of historic interest were not to be damaged.[1] In the event it was a military airship which first reached London, but it fell to the naval airship service to deliver the first great onslaught.

[1] *Der Krieg Zur See*, 1914-1918. Vol. iv, p. 263.

CHAPTER III

THE FIRST RAIDS ON LONDON AND HULL

THE competition between the two German air services for the honour or glory of first reaching London had evidently been keen. Before the army airships had become accustomed to their surroundings in Belgium the ill-fated naval Zeppelin L.8 (Kapitan-leutnant Beelitz) ascended at Dusseldorf on the night of the 26th February, 1915, with instructions to proceed to London. The flight was abandoned owing to strong wind getting up and the L.8 landed amongst her military comrades at Gontrode. She made a second attempt thence on the night of the 4th March, but as has already been told she fell foul of the Belgian gunners at Nieuport in the dawn of the fifth, and with her all hope of the naval service first reaching the coveted objective passed away.

On the last night of May, 1915, England lay on the eastern outskirts of an anti-cyclonic system centred over the Bay of Biscay. The wind was very light from north and north-west; the weather was fine and the moon was at the full. Such were the weather conditions when Hauptmann Linnarz brought his L.Z.38 with a full load of bombs to

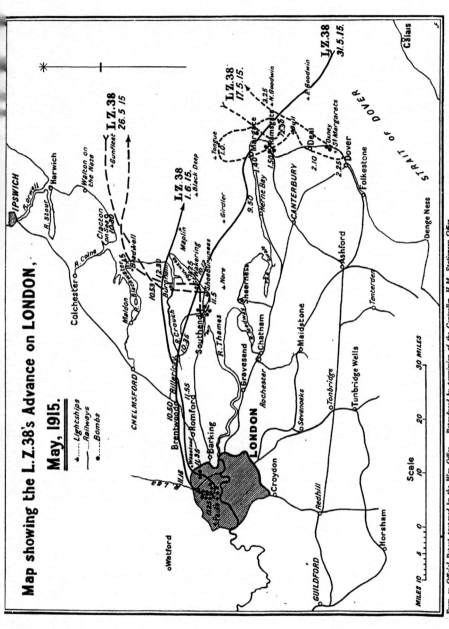

Map showing the L.Z.38's Advance on LONDON, May, 1915.

Legend:
←..... Lightships
—— Railways
●..... Bombs

Scale

MILES 10 5 0   10   20   30 MILES

IPSWICH
R. Orwell
R. Stour
Harwich
Walton on the Naze
Colchester
R. Colne
R. Colne
R. Blackwater
Maldon
Blackwell
Clacton on Sea 10.30
10.53 12.30
Burnham
Gunfleet
L.Z. 38
26.5.15
L.Z. 38
1.6.15.
Black Deep
Maplin
10.35
Wakering
11.25
Southend
Shoeburyness
Girdler
R. Crouch
11.5
R. Thames
11.55
Brentwood
Billericay
Romford
10.50
Wanstead
11.35
Barking
CHELMSFORD
oWatford
9.50
Girdler
Tongue
9.0
R. Thames
Gravesend
Rochester
Chatham
Sheerness
R. Medway
Nore
LONDON
Croydon
Redhill
Horsham
GUILDFORD
Sevenoaks
Tonbridge
Maidstone
Tunbridge Wells
Herne Bay
Margate
2.10
Whitstable
CANTERBURY
Ashford
Tenterden
Y **L.Z. 38**
17.5.15.
3.25
N. Goodwin
Ramsgate
2.35
Deal
Sandwich
2.55
St Margarets
1.40
1.50
1.40
2.51
Dover
Folkestone
Denge Ness
E. Goodwin
L.Z. 38
31.5.15.
Calais
STRAIT OF DOVER

From an Official Report prepared by the War Office. Reproduced by permission of the Controller, H.M. Stationery Office.

This map shows the track of the first German airship to reach London with two preceding attempts. The Zeppelin concerned was the army ship L.Z.38 commanded by Hauptmann Linnarz and operating from Belgium.

The first attempt (not shown on the map) took place at two o'clock in the morning of the 10th May, 1915, when Linnarz reached and bombed Southend. Next in the small hours of the 17th May, 1915, he visited Thanet and bombed Ramsgate and Oxney. Then on the night of the 26th May, 1915, Linnarz paid his second visit to Southend. Finally, on the night of the 31st May, 1915, he reached London, making full use of the experience he had gained in his three previous attempts. Linnarz threw eighty-nine incendiary bombs and thirty grenades on London, as the result of which seven people were killed and thirty-five others were injured.

London. He steered a masterly course. Brushing the coast at Margate and respecting this time the guns at Cliffe, he went straight across the estuary of the Thames and made his landfall north of Shoeburyness; and keeping a course well clear of the river, he traversed Essex and made a claw-like swoop on to the north-eastern segment of the capital. Stoke Newington, Dalston, Hoxton, Shoreditch, Whitechapel, Stepney, West Ham and Leytonstone were freely peppered with incendiary bombs and man-killing grenades.

In all eighty-nine incendiary bombs and thirty grenades were dropped. There were seven fatal casualties and thirty-five people were injured. The raider got clear away, being unmolested save by coastal guns on her arrival and departure. Nine machines went up that night. Unfortunately Flight Lieutenant D. M. Barnes, who left Hendon in a Sopwith, with Flight Sub-Lieutenant B. Travers as observer, crashed at Hatfield. Barnes was killed but Travers escaped with various injuries. Flight Lieutenant A. W. Robertson, who rose from Rochford in a Bleriot, had reached 6,000 feet when he sighted Linnarz's L.Z.38 ahead and above. Robertson inferred that the airship was making for London, so he decided to follow the course of the Thames in an endeavour to intercept the raider. But his engine soon failed and he was compelled to come down. As he could only see water beneath him he decided to land in the soft mud of the river-bank at Leigh.

He was uninjured and managed, with great difficulty, to salve his machine in the dawn of the following day.

Linnarz had a consort that night in the L.Z.37, which appears to have been attacked by aeroplanes off Dunkirk at 9 p.m., but she turned about at the mouth of the Swale on being fired at by the mobile gunners.

An interesting feature of this raid was the height at which it was carried out. No one appears to have seen the airship on her passage to London, and she was only faintly heard by the gun station at Clapton. The race for supremacy in the attainment of the greatest altitudes between the airships on the one hand and the defending aeroplanes and guns on the other had begun.

Linnarz's success brought the naval service again into action. At midday on the 4th June, L.10 (Kapitanleutnant Hirsch) and S.L.3 (Kapitanleutnant Boemack) rose from Nordholz in a slight mist, the former bound for London and the Schutte Lanz for the Humber. About 9 p.m. L.10 bore down from the Outer Gabbard direct to the Isle of Sheppey, and after encircling the mouth of the Swale, she steered an erratic course to Gravesend, over which she described a small figure of eight, turned, and then set a course north-east, making Ipswich in a direct line, and finally passed out to sea by Saxmundham. Her bombs were dropped on Sittingbourne and Gravesend, injuring in all eight persons. While Hirsch was unloading his cargo he was under the impression that he was attacking Harwich. He mistook one of the Thamesmouth lightships for the Cork lightship, from which he said he turned towards Harwich. He identified Harwich and even Ipswich when in reality he was in the neighbourhood of Chatham and Gravesend. Hirsch reported dropping thirty high explosive and ninety incendiary bombs on Harwich. He said:

" These all exploded and all caused fires in the town; moreover, judging by an especially violent explosion, one of the hits must have been on some gasworks or an oil tank. In many places fires broke out, which were visible for a long time." [1]

Actually, the military hospital in the Yacht Club at Gravesend was hit and burnt, as were also a few houses and a stable. S.L.3 was overland for two and a half hours flying very low round the environments of Flamborough Head. She dropped two bombs, one in a field and the other in a garden near Great Driffield. Eight aeroplanes, four naval and four military, were up that night, but failed to see anything of the raiders.

That the army and navy should pool their airship fleets for combined raids on England had been frequently mooted. The main difficulty in the way was due to the fact that the naval and military

[1] *Der Krieg Zur See*, 1914–1918. Vol. iv, p. 174.

airship bases were so far apart. The weather might be promising for a raid at the naval sheds on the north coast of Germany, but totally impossible in Belgium and the Rhineland and vice versa. Further, there was the pride of service, ever jealous of its own arm, which experience has shown militates against smooth co-operation in common tasks. Such points as who is to lead and which service is to issue the orders, etc., always stand in the way of such undertakings. This was by no means peculiar to the German Air Service. It is not surprising, therefore, that such attempts as were made were generally unsuccessful and frequently attended with disastrous results. Take for example the first occasion on which the German naval and military airship services concerted an attack on Great Britain.

On the night of the 6th June, three military airships, L.Z.37 (Oberleutnant van der Haegen), L.Z.38 (Hauptmann Linnarz), and L.Z.39 (Hauptmann Masius), rose from their sheds in Belgium to reinforce and support the naval service in its attack on Great Britain. Linnarz descended almost at once. L.Z.37 and L.Z.39 were unable to make the English coast, probably on account of fog, and turned about for home. At one o'clock in the morning (7th June) the L.Z.37 was detected in the sky over Ostend by Flight Sub-Lieutenant Warneford, whose experience with the L.Z.39 some three weeks before stood him in good stead. He had left Furnes in a Morane monoplane to attack the sheds at Berchem

St. Agathe. Warneford soon caught up the airship, and when near Ghent succeeded in getting into position immediately over her and dropped his bombs. At least one hit fair and square and the Zeppelin burst into flames. The force of the resulting explosion was so great as to upset the equilibrium of Warneford's machine, which in consequence went into a spin. Recovering control, he was compelled to land owing to a broken petrol pipe. Although in enemy territory he managed to repair the defect, restart his engine and get back safely within our lines. Warneford thus gained the distinction of being the first airman to destroy an airship in mid air. For this exploit he won the Victoria Cross. Unfortunately this gallant officer met his death in a trivial accident ten days later.

The same morning Flight Lieutenants J. P. Wilson and J. S. Mills attacked the airship sheds at Evere near Brussels. Wilson arrived in the dark and was challenged by searchlights, to which he replied by a series of flashes from a pocket lamp. These mystic signs apparently satisfied the enemy who did not open fire. Wilson circled round until it was light enough to see the target and then dropped three bombs, the second of which caused a large explosion, clouds of black smoke rising from the shed. Mills now arrived and dropped twelve bombs, after which the whole shed with a Zeppelin inside burst into flames. The Zeppelin was the L.Z.38.

D

If on the eve of these disasters Mathy had known what fate was in store for his military comrades he might not have brought his L.9 from Hage to England with such confidence. His course was such that on nearing the English coast he could choose between two alternatives—whether he should go to London or to Hull. When he arrived at the Wash, visibility was hindered by a thick layer of fog, and a strong headwind made southward progress slow, so that it would scarcely have been possible for him to reach London in the four hours of darkness at his disposal. Consequently Mathy decided to turn towards the Humber. From off Cromer he made straight for Theddlethorpe in Lincoln. From here he kept near the coast, passed the mouth of the Humber, and got to Flamborough Head. Then he turned about and bore down southward straight on Hull, which he reached shortly before midnight. Wavering a little in the mist, the better to fix his position, he passed over the town from which the fog had just lifted. The Sixth Light Cruiser Squadron was lying at anchor under the mist lower down the estuary and H.M.S. *Adventure* docked in Earle's yard for repairs, saw the L.9 and fired at her. On this, Mathy came down to 5,000 feet and went straight for shipping and warehouses. But his bombs, in addition to causing quayside damage, crashed into narrow streets adjoining the docks. The city suffered severely; about forty houses and shops were demolished and many damaged, while a saw mill was burnt out. During the twenty minutes he was over Hull he dropped thirteen high explosive and thirty-nine incendiary bombs. He then made for Grimsby, where he dropped seven incendiary bombs which did little damage. He was fired at by the pom-poms at Immingham and Waltham and so he passed out to sea. Twenty-four folk had been killed in Hull and forty wounded.

Next came the second turn of the Tyne. In the early afternoon of 15th June, in weather conditions particularly favourable for oversea work, the L.10 (Kapitanleutnant Hirsch) and L.11 (Oberleutnant Freiherr von Buttlar) started from Nordholz for England. When ninety nautical miles north-west of Terschelling one of the engines of L.11 broke its crankshaft and the ship turned for home. Hirsch, however, carried on with the Tyne as his objective. He approached the coast at Blyth, well north of his target, obviously to avoid the Tynemouth defences. Otherwise his overland route, although somewhat shorter and more direct, differed little from that followed by Mathy on his visit on 14th April. On making his landfall at half-past eleven he immediately turned south and steered straight for the Tyne. No bombs were wasted in the open country as they were on the former occasion. The first were thrown at Wallsend. Unwarned, many of the Tyneside industrial establishments had their lights at full blaze; syren blasts sounded by H.M.S. *Patrol* as a warning were not understood. Damage was done

to houses and the Eastern marine engineering works.
After bombing Wallsend and the Hebburn collieries
Hirsch turned his attention to Palmer's works at
Jarrow, which presented a perfect target. Seven
high explosive and five incendiary bombs fell on
the engine construction department, causing very
severe damage and great loss of life—seventeen
men were killed and seventy-two were injured.
Before leaving, the airship dropped bombs on
Willington quay, East Howdon, Cookson's antimony
works and Pochin's chemical works. Hirsch went
out to sea via South Shields, leaving a scenic railway
ablaze near the Haxton colliery staithes.

As this raid was conspicuous for accurate bomb
practice on military objectives, Hirsch's report is
worth quoting:

" Shortly after I reached the English coast I
noticed on the portside a great number of lights
and the glare of blast furnaces. Approaching closer,
the course of a river could be distinguished, on the
banks of which were a great number of industrial
works. At this moment the L.10 was suddenly
subjected to heavy fire from various ground batteries.
We were glad to note that shrapnel and not incendiary
shells were being fired. The shrapnel all burst
below the airship. On account of the gunfire I
decided to bomb the locality below the airship as
the many factories and blast furnaces afforded good
targets. In all 2,500 kg. of high explosive and

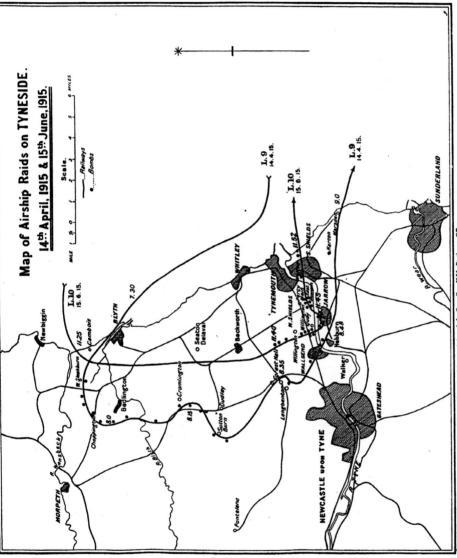

Map of Airship Raids on TYNESIDE.
14th April, 1915 & 15th June, 1915.

Scale.
Railways
Bombs

From an Official Report prepared by the War Office. Reproduced by permission of the Controller, H.M. Stationery Office.

On this map are shown two similar raids on Tyneside by single German naval Zeppelins. On the first occasion on the night of the 14th April, 1915, Kapitänleutnant Mathy raided in the L.9 and dropped bombs pretty freely along his route. The only casualties occurred at Wallsend, where a woman and a child were injured. On the second occasion on the night of the 15th June, 1915, Kapitänleutnant Hirsch came over in the L.10. He carefully preserved his bombs until he reached the industrial establishments on the Tyne. His bomb dropping was remarkably accurate and effective. Extensive damage was done to many works, including Palmer's, at Jarrow, where seventeen men were killed and seventy-two injured.

The German Air Raids on Great Britain, 1914-1918.   Captain Joseph Morris.   Sampson Low.

incendiary bombs were dropped and the effect must have been devastating. By the light of the fires caused by incendiary bombs, the demolition of entire factories, and several explosions, accompanied by an immense glare at the blast furnaces as well as a number of big fires, could clearly be observed. The last four bombs were dropped on a coastal battery which had fired on the airship. The battery did not fire again. The glare from the raided locality was still visible 30 nautical miles away." [1]

Two naval machines rose from Whitley Bay but failed to see anything of Hirsch.

If the raid on London did not give rise to undue alarm, those on Hull and the Tyne demonstrated the defencelessness of the industrial establishments of England. It was represented by prominent citizens that Zeppelins apparently could come when they liked, stay as long as they liked and go when they felt inclined without let or hindrance from anyone on our side. Notwithstanding the fact that the primary object of the raids—the destruction of places of military importance—was a failure, there were important secondary effects. Warnings caused cessation of work and the tense period of standing by with the expectation of bombs dropping at any moment was sufficient to disorganise a works or cause panic. For example, Hull, after Mathy's attack, was half emptied nightly of its poor, who,

[1] *Der Krieg Zur See*, 1914–1918. Vol. iv, pp. 186-187.

after two more scares, refused to stay in the defence-less town and sought refuge in fields as far away as possible.

As a result the Admiralty proceeded with its plan of improving the defences of the north. New stations were opened up at Hornsea, Scarborough and Redcar in the first week in July. The most that the Royal Flying Corps could do was to arrange that in the event of a raid, instructors of training squadrons and pilots of service squadrons, mobilising for overseas, should, if possible, go up and attack the raiders. The task thus imposed on instructors was more than severe. The raids took place by night, and night flying without the necessary ground organization involved considerable danger, so night flights were forbidden except in the event of the arrival of hostile aircraft and practice was consequently greatly restricted.

CHAPTER IV

THE SUMMER RAIDS OF 1915

So far as the Germans were concerned the raids up to now had been tentative and experimental. After their initial failures on the western front, they turned to their beloved instrument and envisaged their frail but formidable Zeppelins breaking down the resistance of the English nation, and so paving the way for easy victory. Their forbears had once before with great secrecy and suddenness seized the coast of Great Britain, and when they found that the London defences barred the way along the Thames they penetrated inland through the estuary of the Humber. Why not ring the changes of history and if the British navy constituted an impenetrable barrier by sea, why not break Britain's insular security by air? The prospects seemed promising; and another fifteen months were to pass before all hopes of crushing England by dirigible airships were irretrievably dashed to the ground by the destruction of the wooden Schutte Lanz over Cuffley, and the might of the airship as an offensive weapon melted away.

The airship attacks next to come evinced for the first time a well-thought-out and progressive programme. The spring raids had been devoted mainly to reconnaissance of the coast and the estuaries of East Anglia and the north-eastern counties. The isolated dash of a military airship to London on the 31st May had shown the possibility of raids on London, and London was the main objective of the raids planned for the anticyclonic periods of the late summer and autumn. Meteorological conditions had now been carefully studied by the enemy, and raids were no longer to be undertaken, as occasionally had happened, in unfavourable weather or during moonlight periods. The method of airship-raiding now settled was to become the normal practice, and very determined efforts were made to launch the attacks with as great a force as possible. General von Falkenhayn urged that to gain effective results a big squadron of airships, accompanied by giant and fighter aeroplanes should be employed as the " point was not to raise the spirits of the German people, but to inflict the maximum damage on the enemy."[1] He proposed that the Chief of the Military Air Forces should be entrusted with the task, the naval and military resources being combined for mammoth attacks on London. But joint action had already been tried and found unsatisfactory and a resumption was strenuously opposed by von Bachmann, the Chief

[1] *Der Krieg Zur See*, 1914–1918. Vol. iv, p. 264.

of the Naval Staff. His reasons were by no means disinterested. The naval air service had acquired several new ships of improved type. The L.10, L.11, L.12 and L.13 were available by August, as were also the S.L.3 and S.L.4, and several others were on the point of delivery. In the same period the army had only acquired the L.Z.72 and L.Z.74, and owing to severe losses they had not sufficient capital to impose their will on the project. So that it fell to the German naval air service to carry out the first attack on London in force. They were ready in August and started on the first favourable opportunity.

When the great attack was planned Strasser proposed to use the newest ships, viz. L.10, L.11, L.12, L.13 and L.14 for London and L.9, S.L.3 and S.L.4 for the easier targets between the Humber and the Tyne. The older ships, L.6, L.7 and P.L.25, were to be restricted to reconnaissance with L.9, S.L.3 and S.L.4 in emergencies. The date chosen was 9th August. The raid was unfortunate from the beginning, as on the appointed day British light cruisers were nearing the end of the hunt of the German minelayer *Meteor* off the Heligoland Bight. She had been warned by the airships L.7 and P.L.25 as to Commodore Tyrwhitt's enveloping movement, and realising that escape was impossible her commander decided to scuttle his ship. The fate of the *Meteor* may have played its part in rendering the London attack ineffective.

L.9, L.12 and L.13 left Hage about eleven o'clock in the morning and radiated into the Bight presumably on preliminary reconnaissance. At 12.32 p.m. Strasser asked the admiral commanding the German fleet for instructions with regard to the projected raid. The admiral decided that in L.7 and P.L.25 he had sufficient aerial support, and the raid was to take place and be carried out by the five newest Zeppelins. Accordingly L.10 and L.11 set out from Nordholz to join their consorts, all five ships being summoned to rendezvous twenty nautical miles north of Borkum. L.9 was detailed for the Humber whilst the remainder were to proceed in formation towards the English coast, setting a course slightly to the north of Harwich. All this according to Groos. We are informed that at 7.30 p.m. Strasser gave the following orders by searchlight signal:

" Remain together until 8.45 p.m., then each airship will carry out an independent raid, first on the London docks, then the city. For the attack, follow a more or less westerly course, then turn northwards and retire in a north-easterly direction." [1]

So far as the main objective was concerned the raid was a complete failure. Only one vessel—the L.10—got within thirty miles of London. Oberleutnant Wenke, her commander, reported that he had reached his objective and was so accredited. Actually he made his landfall at Aldeburgh, rounded

[1] *Der Krieg Zur See*, 1914–1918. Vol. iv, p. 264.

Framlingham and flew parallel to the Great Eastern
main line.   When nearing Chelmsford he seems
to have lost the railway and turned to the south-east,
which course brought him to the Isle of Sheppey.
Here in the belief that he had reached London he
dropped all his bombs, twenty-two high explosive
(of which two were of 100 kg. weight) and sixty
incendiary.   Of those which fell on *terra firma* we
counted only eight high explosive and six incendiary.
The bombs which he says were intended for shipping
did no other damage than breaking a few windows
at Eastchurch. L.11 (Oberleutnant Freiherr von
Buttlar) brushed the coast between Southwold and
Lowestoft, where he dropped some dozen bombs
which killed one woman and injured seven other
persons and wrecked or damaged a few houses.
He reported bombing Harwich, and of the naval
six-pounder which engaged him he says:

" The salvoes were relatively close to the airship
and one shell burst close below the forward car."

It was to escape this fire that he hurriedly dropped
his load of bombs on Lowestoft and got as near his
ceiling as possible and out seawards at full speed.
Mathy, in the L.13, took no part in the attack as
his forward engine broke down when he was at the
mouth of the Thames and he turned back.   He
believed that he was north of Harwich and had
witnessed Buttlar's mythical attack there, whilst

actually he saw Wenke's London bombs falling on Eastchurch.

The prize ship of the night was the L.12. We thought that Oberleutnant Peterson had attacked Dover by design and not by mistake. When he was off the shore, between Margate and Herne Bay, he thought a strong south wind had blown him far north of Harwich and that he was between the Haisboro' lightship and Winterton. So he turned for south and after a zig-zag path reached Dover soon after midnight, believing that he had now found Harwich. He had unwittingly wandered into a veritable hornets' nest. As he was dropping his bombs on the harbour he was suddenly assailed by massed anti-aircraft guns and his ship was hit at once, notwithstanding his attempt to reach his ceiling. His bombs were unavailing and wrought little damage. The injury the airship had received proved serious. She made for Belgium, but was losing gas and was compelled to descend gradually to the surface of the water, and when a few miles off Zeebrugge was picked up and taken in tow by a German torpedo boat. She was towed to Ostend and was made fast to the quay during the morning of the 10th. Flight Commander J. R. Smyth-Pigott had gone up from Dunkirk at half-past eight in a B.E.2c to look for the crippled raider. He found her to seaward, three miles off Ostend, in the process of being hauled down by the destroyer which had taken her in tow. He attacked with two twenty-pound

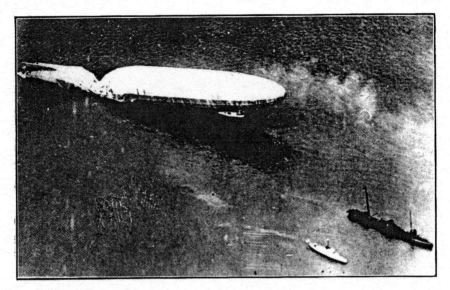

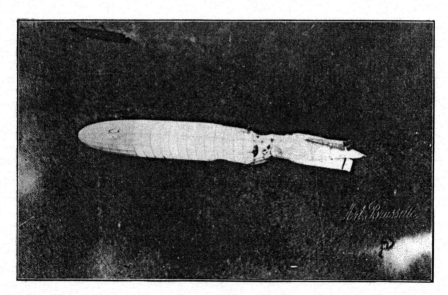

The Zeppelin L.12 on the sea off Ostend after being hit by the Dover guns during the raid on the night of the 9th August, 1915   *To face p.* 46

bombs and six grenades from a height of 500 feet under heavy fire from enemy destroyers on the scene and also from the shore batteries. When he saw that the L.12's back was broken Smyth-Pigott decided to return. Next a procession from Dunkirk to Ostend was instituted to finish off Peterson's ill-fated vessel. Unfortunately, Flight Lieutenant D. K. Johnston failed to return. He was shot down and killed. Only a few fragments of the L.12 could be salved by the Germans. She paid the highest price faulty navigation imposes on its victims.

Remains the old L.9; she was the only ship which got anywhere near the objective. Kapitanleutnant Loewe, her commander, was unfortunate in his landfall. He appeared directly over the newly-established naval air station at Atwick, near Hornsea, one of the three which had been brought into existence to deal with northern raiders. His height was estimated at some 3,000 feet. Two machines rose from the station in pursuit and the airship shot up to about 10,000 feet and stopped her engines apparently to listen for the aeroplanes. On their approach she steered eastward out to sea and was lost in the fog. Ten minutes later she reappeared to the northward at Fraisthorpe, near Bridlington, but again went out to sea and was next seen off Hornsea again going north. A naval aeroplane again rose from Atwick and the airship promptly went out to sea again, followed for some thirty-five minutes by the machine. She was at sea for about an hour and came in again at Aldeburgh shortly after 10 p.m. She struck the railway at Hutton-Cranswick and turned south evidently with the intention of making Hull. She lost her way and finally reached Goole whose lights she discerned in the fog. After bombing Goole the airship rounded Selby and finally passed out over Hornsea. Loewe went home with the certainty that he had bombed Hull, but mathematicians would grant him a first approximation.

Of the many airmen up that night in England, Flight Sub-Lieutenant R. Lord rose from Westgate in a Sopwith to attack a Zeppelin seen approaching from Herne Bay. The airship appeared to turn north-east simultaneously with the departure of the aeroplane and was lost to sight and hearing. Flares and searchlights were then lit to assist the pilot to land and soon after the machine was heard descending. It struck the ground, however, fifty yards short and crashed. Unfortunately Lord was fatally injured.

The performance of the 9th August was not improved upon three days later. Of four starters only one reached England to raid. L.10 (Oberleutnant Wenke) came in at Lowestoft at about 9.30 p.m. and after a tortuous path reached Woodbridge, having just before dropped some flares and incendiary bombs. Woodbridge received four high explosive and twenty incendiary missiles in reply to machine-gun and rifle-fire and from the 2nd/3rd London Infantry Brigade. Some more bombs were dropped near Ipswich, and the airship was then attracted to Harwich by lights in the harbour which were put on to enable a squadron of destroyers to enter and take up moorings. Dropping her remaining few bombs on the outskirts of Harwich the L.10 followed the coast to Aldeburgh and then went out to sea. According to Wenke's report Harwich, " though well darkened," was recognised from the outline of the coast and " the electric power station and railway stood out particularly clearly in the thin air." [1]

L.11 (Oberleutnant Freiherr von Buttlar) was this night something of a mystery ship. According to Groos, the L.11 when in sight of the coast near Orfordness, fell out with engine breakdown and took no further part. An airship, believed to be the L.11, however, was made out by us as having come down from off Harwich to Thanet by an S path and then to have made a figure of eight, one loop over the Thames estuary and the other over east Kent, before she disappeared without having dropped any bombs. Von Buttlar that night was to have a trying adventure. He reported that on his homeward journey, when N.W. of Texel, he suddenly found himself cut off from home by a heavy advancing thunderstorm. Groos says:

" The centre of the storm appeared to be over Terschelling and was rapidly approaching the airship.

Der Krieg Zur See, 1914–1918. Vol. iv, p. 268

An attempt to fly round it, keeping an easterly course proved unsuccessful and even in trying to get round to the north of it the airship was caught by the storm over the Dogger Bank. The rain and heavy squalls drove the airship down to 300 metres altitude from time to time, whilst the lightning came closer and closer. It was impossible to proceed further northwards on account of petrol shortage and equally impossible to delay any further in pushing through to the east. Scarcely had this course been embarked upon than the airship found herself in the centre of the storm. Lightning ran at intervals of five seconds from cloud to cloud, and cloud to water and encompassed the airship, the points and wire stays of which emitted electric sparks. Bluish flames 30 centimetres long ran along the machine guns and even the crew on the top platform who were soaked with rain, were encircled in a ring of light. Had the airship been carried above her pressure height by a squall, gas given off, and inflammable gas formed the airship would have perished by fire. She survived all danger, however, though the storm lasted until 3 a.m., and at 7.37 a.m. (August 13th) landed safely at Nordholz." [1]

Four machines rose that night. One saw nothing through the rain and mist and three landed with engine trouble.

The naval airship campaign against London

[1] *Der Krieg Zur See*, 1914–1918. Vol. iv, p. 269.

launched with such vigour in the summer of 1915, had as yet been feeble and ineffective and the coveted objective had only been reached in imagination, but on the night of the 17th August, Wenke was to attain it in reality. He brought his L.10 to Sizewell Gap and just before nine o'clock came inland over Shingle Street. He picked up the Great Eastern main line south of Ipswich and followed it to Chelmsford. He then struck west to Waltham Abbey, dropped a petrol tank at Ongar, and made his approach to London from the north. He had been fired at at various points on his route but he reserved his bombs until he reached Walthamstow. His main cargo was discharged on Leyton and a few missiles were dropped on Leytonstone and Wanstead flats. He then more or less retraced his steps, shedding two bombs at Chelmsford on the way and passed out to sea soon after midnight. Twenty-one high explosive and twenty-four incendiary bombs were counted. In all ten persons were killed and forty-eight injured. The material damage was mainly to small private houses, Leyton railway station and a Wesleyan chapel. He appears to have mistaken a model yacht pond at Wanstead flats for the Thames, as at the time he was over it, according to the German official account:

" Between Blackfriars Bridge and London Bridge the Commandant gave the order to attack and 20 H.E.

E

bombs and 40 incendiary bombs were dropped, the effect of which was manifested by the collapse of buildings and the outbreak of big fires." [1]

An airship which was made out to be the L.11 crossed the coast that night at Herne Bay, about 9.30 p.m. She came in low over the pier from the sea but rose on being fired at by men of the 42nd Provisional Battalion. She flew to Canterbury, Ashford, Faversham and Whitstable, going out to sea again near her original landfall. She had spent some two hours overland at times under rifle fire. The anti-aircraft gun at Faversham was unable to come into action owing to the current for the searchlight being cut off in order not to betray the powder works. The L.11 dropped in all eighteen high explosive and forty-four incendiary bombs, but they fell for the most part in open country and did little damage.

According to the official German account the L.11 that night bombed the Eastern quarter of London under heavy anti-aircraft fire on either side of the Thames. [2]

L.14 (Kapitanleutnant Böcker) steered an erratic course off Great Yarmouth, being within sight for some three hours. According to Groos:

" L.14 from an altitude of 2,550 metres dropped 50 incendiary and 20 H.E. bombs on the blast furnaces

[1] *Der Krieg Zur See*, 1914–1918. Vol. iv, pp. 275–276.
[2] *Der Krieg Zur See*, 1914–1918. Vol. iv, p. 276.

and factory premises in the vicinity of Ipswich and
Woodbridge, after the airship, on account of repeated
trouble with two of her engines, had given up the
idea of a raid on London.   Whilst the bombs were
being dropped all the engines except one gave
trouble, so that the airship dropped to an altitude of
1,250 metres.   Immediately after this two more of
the engines began to run again, so the L.14 quickly
climbed to 2,400 metres and in this way was able, at
the eleventh hour, to evade the heavy guns and
machine-gun fire which was opened without any
assistance from searchlights, immediately the airship began to drop her bombs." [1]

Actually his bombs were dropped in the sea, one
near the Cross Sand lightship, and in addition Böcker
came down and potted at a little steamer with
machine-gun fire.

Six machines went up.   Five saw nothing of the
enemy.   One from Chelmsford, piloted by Flight
Sub-Lieutenant C. D. Morrison, saw a Zeppelin but
lost it.   On landing, the machine was blown to
pieces by the explosion of its own bombs.   Morrison
was injured but his observer, Flight Sub-Lieutenant
H. H. Square, was unhurt.

[1] *Der Krieg Zur See*, 1914–1918. Vol. iv, p. 276.

CHAPTER V

MEANWHILE, the acquisition of new ships and the exploits of the navy brought about a recrudescence of the military service. On the night of the 7th September, three military airships suddenly appeared over England all bound for London; and two did in fact reach the objective, and the third very nearly. They came from the Belgian sheds and no intimation whatsoever had been received that a raid was impending. L.Z.77 (Hauptmann Horn) got to Hatfield shortly after midnight, turned back and went home via Lowestoft undetected by two naval pilots, who had risen from Yarmouth. Explosions at sea from the direction she had taken may have resulted from bombs aimed at shipping. Such bombs as were dropped overland fell in open country and did no damage. At the time she turned about, searchlights were sweeping the London skies for L.Z. 74 (Hauptmann George) and S.L.2 (Hauptmann von Wobeser). George passed clean across the capital from north to south. Fortunately for London he had previously unloaded his bombs on the glasshouses at Cheshunt, and so when he was fair and square over the city he had only one incendiary bomb to spare and this fell on a store near Fenchurch street.

The Schutte Lanz's itinerary was almost perfect. She struck the coast at the mouth of the Crouch flying low, and followed the Great Eastern line into London. She reached Leytonstone shortly before midnight, turned south, and when over the Isle of Dogs threw her first bombs, subsequently scattering her load over the south-eastern part of London. She then made for her exit at Harwich where she met the L.Z.74, and they went out to sea in company side by side, having during the raid rarely been out of each other's sight. The Schutte Lanz had discharged on London eighteen high explosive and twenty-six incendiary bombs. Six men, six women and six children were killed and thirty-eight persons were injured. The material damage was slight and in the main was confined to private houses. S.L.2 reached home, but not safely. She crashed at Berchem and took no further part in raiding England. This, the second occasion, was to be the last on which military airships were to penetrate the inner London atmosphere.

The military success brought the navy into the field the very next day. L.11, L.13 and L.14 set out to attack London on 8th September, while the L.9 was again detailed for the north. L.11 (Oberleutnant Freiherr von Buttlar) went back almost at once with engine trouble. The others carried on.

The L.14 (Kapitanleutnant Böcker) simply penetrated a little way into Norfolk, spent her bombs on Bylaugh Park and East Dereham, turned about and made off. L.9 (Kapitanleutnant Loewe) came in shortly after nine o'clock between Whitby and Kettleness. Passing up the coast she dropped occasional bombs. Her main load was dropped at Skinningrove, being evidently aimed at the explosive works there. One fell plumb on the cover of a huge tank of T.N.T., but fortunately failed to explode. If it had done so there is no doubt that the entire factory would have been destroyed. After circling above the works the airship made off.

The glow of the iron ore slag on the cliffs at Skinningrove was frequently used at night by German airship commanders as a means of getting their bearings when approaching England from the sea. This guiding light was not exactly appreciated by them and Skinningrove received a frequent shower of bombs. A large percentage, however, were " duds " and to this fact the factory mainly owed its escape from destruction or even serious damage.

Now for Mathy. He brought his L.13 to the Wash, and without wasting time or ammunition, swooped down straight on London, which he reached at about eleven o'clock, and at once began his onslaught. Golders Green, possibly on account of its proximity to Hendon aerodrome, received the first bombs. Thereafter he indulged in promiscuous practice, his missiles falling in the centre of the capital and the city. Mathy's fifteen high explosive, including one weighing 300 kg., and fifty-five incendiary bombs inflicted enormous material damage (from the point of view of value) on the hapless city, probably the greatest of any raid. Twenty-two persons were killed and eighty-seven injured, the death roll being swelled by the destruction of two motor-omnibuses.

The L.13 had been picked up by searchlight and twenty-six guns in and around London opened fire on her, but apparently without scoring a hit. Aeroplanes which ascended from Yarmouth had long ago landed when Mathy passed thence out to sea. According to the German official account, Mathy, when on his course to London, via King's Lynn and Cambridge, found the lighted villages and towns on the rising slopes above the low-lying ground afforded the best possible assistance in finding bearings, and the glare of London was recognisable at Cambridge. He found that at just over 10,000 feet he was safe from the numerous shells which were being fired at him, whilst below that height he had almost been hit several times. Groos informs us that:

" In spite of the good results obtained the anti-aircraft defence was so extensive that the commander of the airship, in his report, stated that in future with clear sky, airships would only be able to remain quite a short while over the city and that it would be hardly possible to seek out special objectives." [1]

Seven machines rose that night. Three from Redcar failed to find Loewe. Likewise three from Yarmouth sought in vain for Böcker and Mathy. In addition, Flight Sub-Lieutenant V. Nicholl ascended at dusk, in a seaplane, from the trawler *Kingfisher*, some forty miles out to sea, east of Yarmouth. It was very misty and he saw nothing. Unfortunately there was a fatal casualty. Flight Sub-Lieutenant G. W. Hilliard went up from Yarmouth shortly after eight and after a two hours patrol came down to land at Bacton. He crashed into a field adjoining the aerodrome and was killed by the explosion of his own bombs. Flight Sub-Lieutenant J. M. Cripps from the same station had an alarming adventure. He rose just before eight. An hour later his engine failed and he was compelled to land. In the darkness, intensified by mist, Cripps could not see to choose a landing place in the limited time at his disposal. His gravest fear was that if he crashed his bombs would explode, so that when his altimeter showed 100 feet he stepped out on to a wing but retained control of his machine. Judging the time that it would take for the aeroplane to reach the ground, he allowed six seconds and jumped clear. He fell on his shoulder in some soft marsh and was unhurt, while the machine landed itself practically intact.

[1] *Der Krieg Zur See*, 1914–1918. Vol. iv, pp. 285-286.

Two successive nocturnal visits by isolated airships on the nights of the 11th and 12th September completed the military contribution to the 1915 campaign. On the former occasion a fairly wide sweep was made of Essex, Suffolk and Norfolk. The raid was undoubtedly intended for London, and judging by the large number of incendiary bombs dropped, the commander apparently proposed to burn the city down, but he got no nearer than North Weald Bassett, which received his missiles without, however, suffering any damage or casualties. On the following night little more than the coast of Essex and Suffolk was passed over. Some twenty-two high explosives and five incendiary bombs were dropped on villages between Colchester and Woodbridge. There were no casualties and only a few panes of glass were broken. Both raiders encountered fog, which probably accounts for their feeble efforts. On both these occasions single naval machines had risen in fruitless search for the solitary airships.

The last raid of September and the penultimate of the year took place on the next night (13th September), when the naval airships L.11, L.13, L.14 came again once more bound for London. L.11 (Oberleutnant von Buttlar) turned back when thirty nautical miles from the coast. L.14 (Kapitanleutnant Böcker) also turned back without crossing the coast. Only one ship actually raided. The L.13 (Kapitanleutnant Mathy) came in near Harwich shortly before midnight. Mathy intended to repeat his performance of the 8th, but a thunderstorm sent him into the clouds. On emerging he found himself above Harwich and made ready for London, but according to his account he was heavily fired on from practically vertically below, a shell passing clean through two gasbags. He then hurriedly dropped his bombs in the open, jettisoned all possible paraphernalia and made for home. When he landed at Hage his ship struck the ground and was still further damaged. But we are informed repairs were effected on four days. Felixstowe's six-pounder fired twelve rounds and the naval mobile section at Levington Heath fired some hundred Maxim rounds at Mathy, but they did not know of their success. Two naval machines up from Dover failed to sight the raiders.

We appear to have no version of the next raid. According to German official account, von Buttlar in the L.11 appears to have set off for a raid on London on the night of the 15th September, 1915. Quoting Groos:

" Headwind, low cloud and high temperature, made headway and climb to a high altitude difficult and at 9.15 p.m. L.11, when at an altitude of 1,700 metres close to the English coast off Haisborough, on a star shell signal being fired by a ship, was suddenly fired on from all sides by ships with screened lights. These ships had not been observed before and had evidently purposely allowed the airship to come close in. Though four petrol tanks were immediately slipped, this was not enough to allow the airship to climb to a safe altitude owing to the high temperature, so that the bombs carried had to be dropped without selecting any special objective on the ships and on four guns on the coast which opened fire practically simultaneously with the dropping of the first bomb. A huge column of fire and two specially loud explosions, however, showed that the airship's bombs had had a certain effect. Although the airship quickly climbed to 2,750 metres, and in consequence of the sharp angle of climb the forward engine failed temporarily, she was unable to shake off the enemy for 10 minutes. Landing was effected at Nordholz shortly after 3 a.m." [1]

Meanwhile, what of home defences? When one looks back on those troublous times and views things in their true perspective, the wonder is not that so little was done, but that so much was accomplished. Those who so lightly blamed the navy little knew how well they were being protected. To every action there is reaction and the British navy has always given as good as it has received. The successful offensive against the German Zeppelin had hindered, retarded and thwarted many a vicious project. The German raider, if he got across,

[1] *Der Krieg Zur See*, 1914–1918. Vol. iv, pp. 295–296.

learned to dread the navy's guns with mortal fear;
and who will ever know what terrible trials were
averted by those brave airmen, who rose from
fog-enveloped aerodromes with little prospect of
ever reaching earth again alive? Many a time the
report " nothing seen " would be rendered; but
seeing nothing themselves they were frequently
seen by their prey and so frustrated many a
raider. If a list of unknown heroes were being
compiled these would assuredly figure amongst the
first.

The navy, however, had their hands full. The
enemy submarine campaign was steadily gaining
in force and effect, and more and more aircraft were
required to deal with a menace far more serious than
air raids on England. They had no longer sufficient
resources to deal with aerial home defence, particularly if this duty should absorb a number of
aeroplanes which were most urgently required for
the fleet. The true sphere of naval aircraft was the
sea; the location and destruction of hostile submarines was the paramount duty. Next came
overseas reconnaissance for locating hostile ships,
then spotting and observation work for warships
against shore forces, and finally attacks of hostile
aircraft overseas. In the order of things it was
the duty of the army to protect the soil against
hostile forces of whatever element, once they had
penetrated inland, and if the navy had carried this
burden for over a year it was time for the army

to resume their responsibility. This they had provisionally agreed to do in the new year, but meanwhile the raids were getting more and more formidable and immediate action was pressing. So long as the responsibility remained with the Admiralty it was to be carried out to the fullest capacity. Aerial home defence had become too vast a problem to be dealt with by a sub-department, so on 12th September, 1915, a flag officer was appointed with direct responsibility to the Board of Admiralty for the anti-aircraft defence of London. This officer was Sir Percy Scott. In this appointment is reflected the faith of the navy in the gun, and who shall say that this at that time was not the best policy? True, an airship had been destroyed in mid-air by an aeroplane, but this was in the light of day and an exceptional performance. On the other hand several airships had already been hit by guns at night, one at least to its ultimate destruction, and shells were respected to the utmost by those against whom they were directed. Informed naval opinion was to the effect that the main defence of London was by guns and searchlights, patrolling aircraft being secondary. If aeroplanes were only subsidiary the navy could continue to bear the burden of defending Great Britain with guns, and so wavered a bit as the time approached for the transfer.

Sir Percy Scott immediately got down to the job. He urged that a fleet of at least a hundred aeroplanes

armed with guns, should be got ready and pilots to
man them well trained in night-flying and attack.
He even thought that it would be good policy
to build at once a score of large rigid airships capable
of not only attacking and defeating Zeppelins,
but of retaliating on German towns. This project
he suggested should be well advertised. He strongly
represented that unless the raiders were checked
we might be prevented from winning the war, and
he pressed that the manufacture of anti-Zeppelin
guns should receive priority over all other orders.
He put on order more guns and unearthed neglected
weapons of all kinds; guns made for Greece or
Brazil, an experimental gun abandoned at Woolwich
and guns which he won from the fleet. New
stations were hastily sited and were being erected
within a week of his charge. He asked for and
obtained reports on the aerial defences of Paris,
and he sent an officer over to procure a specimen
French mobile 75 mm. gun and to arrange for a
consignment of thirty others. The first arrived in
time for the raid on the 13th October which was
very severely to test our defences.

So far as the army was concerned, such aeroplanes
and anti-aircraft guns as were available or awaiting
to go overseas were used in co-operation whenever
possible. In particular aeroplanes at military
stations in the vicinity of London—at Hounslow,
Northolt and Joyce Green—were kept ready, and
landing grounds had been established at Blackheath,

Romford, Farningham and Wimbledon. At each
station a pilot was detailed daily for night duty in
the event of a raid.

It was now fairly clear that while there were two
air services whichever was charged with the responsibility it would have to be assisted by the other.
But the fundamental policy, that is to say the strategy
to be employed, was largely dependent on the
responsible partner. The navy looked upon the
gun as the premier defence, but the army, whilst
not being dogmatic, considered that in the aeroplane
was to be found the chief counter to the Zeppelin,
and that up to that time the aeroplane had not had
a fair chance. Many attempts were made to for-
mulate schemes of co-operation and some were as
obscure as the most forensic document. Broadly,
the Admiralty wished to be limited to the coast
region and that the War Office should guard London
and all other towns not within twenty miles of the
coast, and such military-defended ports within the
twenty mile limit as might be arranged. The army,
on the other hand, did not think it practicable to
attempt to delimit the respective responsibilities by
an arbitrary line at a given distance from the coast.
They were of the opinion that it would be far better
if the navy were to undertake to deal with all hostile
aircraft attempting to reach this country, whilst
the army undertook to deal with all such craft which
succeeded in reaching these shores, and that all
defence arrangements on land should be undertaken

by the army, who would also provide the aeroplanes required to work with the home defence troops, and to protect garrisons and vulnerable areas. In the event this scheme was agreed to by the navy and the duty of naval aircraft in Great Britain was to be restricted to co-operation with the fleet and coast patrol flotillas and for coast watching. Two more raids, both of a serious nature, one on London and the other on the Midlands, were to take place before the issue was joined and the responsibility passed back to the War Office to remain with them to the end.

CHAPTER VI

FROM LONDON TO THE MIDLANDS

THE German military airship command by now was becoming somewhat chastened. We learn from Groos that the Chief of the General Staff of the armies in the field had approached the Chief of the Naval Staff with the request that

" For the time being only the docks and wharves of London should be raided and that the town itself should not be bombed so long as the enemy refrained from raiding the open towns in Germany."

But the Chief of the Naval Staff was unable to give his full approval

" in the interests of the conduct of naval warfare and in view of the importance of the air raids on the city,"

but he gave orders that

" In the future, air raids should be restricted once more as far as possible to those parts of London on the banks of the Thames, as to which no restriction had been made by the German authorities, and that the northern quarter of the city inhabited chiefly by the poorer classes should as far as possible be avoided."

For the darker nights of October, raids were planned for Liverpool, but we are given to understand that the weather conditions for this project were not suitable; so the order was London as usual. Accordingly on the 13th October, five naval airships—L.11, L.13, L.14, L.15 and L.16—set out for the attack. There seems to have been a very distinct, tactical plan underlying this raid, which was carried out in proper squadron formation. When within an hour's journey of the coast, Mathy, who was leading the formation, issued the following order by wireless in order to prevent collisions in fog or mist:

" Course during raid E.N.E. Course during retreat N.E. Immediately after raid report by W/T; altitude, name of commander."[1]

Four ships reached the vicinity of the coast together and waited for one another between the Haisboro' and Would lightships. They then crossed at Bacton practically at the same time, 6.30 p.m. Buttlar, however, in the L.11, did not come in till an hour later. The L.13, L.14, L.15, L.16, when overland steered similar courses up to Thetford.

[1] *Der Krieg Zur See*, 1914–1918. Vol. iv, p. 335.

Thence L.15 (Kapitanleutnant Breithaupt) and L.16 (Oberleutnant Peterson) continued at about an hour's interval in a direct course towards London, while L.13 (Kapitanleutnant Mathy) and L.14 (Kapitanleutnant Böcker) laid their courses in nutcracker fashion so as to envelop the City and attack it from south-west and south-east respectively.

Breithaupt, in the L.15, alone got plumb over the target, having stuck to his course. He cut across London almost from west to east between 9 and 10 p.m. Peterson apparently got no farther than Chipping Ongar, where he turned for Ware at the time Breithaupt was vertically over London. His main load of bombs was dropped at Hertford, whose lights attracted his attention. He returned with the report that he had bombed London. Meanwhile, Mathy in the L.13 swept round by St. Albans, Watford, Uxbridge, Staines and so to Guildford, where he twisted about, momentarily lost. Then he resumed his outer circle, passed Redhill, then on to Bromley and next Woolwich, which he reached shortly before midnight. Böcker, in the L.14, on the other hand, bore down south almost in a straight line from Thetford to Hythe. Rounding the Romney marshes he passed to Winchelsea, whence he altered course to Tunbridge Wells and so to Croydon, which he reached at 11.20 p.m.

Mathy, Böcker and Breithaupt on their outward journey made for Aldeburgh, north of which they passed out, but Peterson went back to Bacton. In spite of Mathy's precautions, disaster nearly befell the raid. Curiously enough it was his own ship which almost collided with Böcker's on two occasions; first near Oxted at about 11 p.m., when their paths crossed and the second, half an hour later, when over Bromley where again they met. The new mobile anti-aircraft guns firing from freshly-selected positions well clear of London came into action for the first time, with the result that L.13 was attacked by gunfire near Hatfield and similarly L.15 near Broxbourne. Further, the newly installed mobile guns opened fire at Loughton, Romford, Hainault and Sutton's farms, and on the river at the Royal Albert dock and Plumstead, causing consider able trouble to L.13 and L.14 on their departure from London. Five machines in all went up from Joyce Green, Hainault and Sutton's farms and only one pilot saw an airship in the searchlights. Two were crashed on landing, but they played their part

" Even more sinister was the appearance of another danger in addition to the anti-aircraft guns," says the German official account of Breithaupt's experience.

" Four aeroplanes, at first observed by the flame from the exhaust and then clearly shown up in the beams of the searchlights endeavoured to reach the airship and shoot her down with incendiary ammunition. They approached within 1,000 metres, then within 500 metres, and not until the L.15 had dropped all her ballast was she out of reach of the enemy."[1]

Now for von Buttlar with his L.11. He reported being fired at by the ubiquitous "ships with screened lights," and that he, therefore, decided to turn south to fly along the coast while his comrades went by the inland route. He then described how he reached Woolwich via the Thames and there dropped his bombs which gave rise to " violent explosions " and fires. However, an airship which we thought to be the L.11 got no farther than Norwich, having hurriedly dropped bombs on Norfolk villages on the way, the damage incurred being mostly broken windows. She then went due east out to sea and was lost to sight. She was fired at by machine-gunners at Bacton, and this apparently diverted her from penetrating further inland. On her outward journey she was engaged by artillery without success.

On the whole the raid proved serious. The casualties caused, if considered from the point of view of the total number of ships employed and of bombs expended, were more severe than in any other airship raid before or after. Breithaupt reserved most of his bombs until well over the centre of the City, and dropped them on Exeter street, Wellington street (between the Lyceum theatre and the offices of the *Morning Post*), on Catherine

[1] *Der Krieg Zur See*, 1914–1918. Vol. iv, pp. 336–337.

street, Aldwych, the Royal Courts of Justice, Carey
street, Lincoln's Inn, Chancery lane, Holborn,
Gray's Inn, Hatton Garden and Farringdon road.
In all, nineteen high explosive and eleven incendiary
bombs fell from his ship on London. Croydon
also suffered severely from eighteen bombs which
Böcker threw there. Further, many of Mathy's
missiles, mainly incendiary, were dropped at Woolwich, causing damage to barracks there and to some
shops in the arsenal. In all, for the five ships we
counted 102 high explosive and 87 incendiary bombs
dropped. The total casualties of the raid were
71 killed and 128 injured. London alone suffered
38 killed and 87 injured.

This raid—the last of 1915—presents a few
interesting features. With the approach of the
season, when the prevailing weather appeared most
favourable for airships attacking London, those
charged with the defence of the capital were seriously
concerned. When such an attack became imminent
it was feared that airships would probably avoid
the eastern defences and make a descent from the
north. Accordingly, special strategical dispositions
were made to meet and engage any raiders which
might attempt such a manœuvre. On the 1st
October orders were issued for guns, searchlights
and aeroplanes to be brought to the vicinity of
London as a precautionary measure of an experimental nature. Two Essex farms near London
were impressed for aerodromes for the period,

Damage done to the Strand Theatre when two bombs were dropped in Aldwych by the Zeppelin L.15 on the night of the 13th October, 1915. A previous bomb from the same airship fell in front of the Lyceum Theatre   *To face p.* 72

4th to the 12th October. One was Sutton's farm, situated some two miles to the south-west of Hornchurch. The other was Hainault farm, by Hainault forest, and some four miles to the north-west of Romford. These were designated for the time being as landing grounds Nos. 2 and 3 respectively. Needless to say, once the War Office had planted their machines on these farms, the occupation extended for the " duration." Such were the beginnings of the two most famous aerodromes to figure in the defence of London. Six of the very best machines available—B.E.2C's—were distributed, two apiece, at Northolt aerodrome, at Hainault and at Sutton's farm. In addition a B.E.2C and an S.E.4A were kept ready at Joyce Green. On Zeppelins approaching London, each of the grounds would be informed as to the sending up of machines. Pilots were to patrol in the vicinity of their aerodromes for one and a half hours at 8,000 feet unless hostile aircraft were sighted, in which case they were to take the necessary steps to engage them. To assist the defending pilots in their quest for the nocturnal visitors, searchlights were installed near the aerodromes. Corresponding dispositions of mobile thirteen-pounder guns were also made. The experiment was to end on the morning of the 13th, but as the anticipated raid did not come off, instructions were issued to the officers in charge of the guns to pack up and return to Woolwich. In the afternoon, however, secret orders were issued for

them to proceed to other positions previously
reconnoitred instead of moving into Woolwich.
This they did, with the result that every mobile
gun was engaged when the attack took place.
Similarly the aeroplanes were retained at the farms,
there to remain. It is quite possible that our change
of plans at the eleventh hour upset the enemy's
calculations.

With regard to the sinister menace referred to
by Breithaupt, it may be of interest to record the
doings that night of the aviators who watched over
London. Lieutenant F. H. Jenkins went up at
eight o'clock from Hainault farm, and after half an
hour saw heavy gunfire to the north of London.
He made in that direction, but although he searched
for an hour and a half at a height of 8,000 feet, he
saw nothing to indicate the presence of the enemy.
The fog was so intense that as low as a hundred feet
he was unable to see the aerodrome flares; consequently he landed short and his machine struck a
hedge. He was uninjured; his aeroplane was only
slightly damaged. Soon after he had landed an
airship passed overhead, whereupon Lieutenant C. E.
Wardle ascended. After a fruitless hour and a
quarter's patrol, Wardle came down to land, but
like Jenkins he could not see the flares and crashed.
He also escaped injury. From Sutton's farm rose
Second Lieutenent J. C. Slessor. He went up in
the mist about half-past nine, and when at some
2,500 feet, saw a Zeppelin held in a searchlight

beam to the east, but only momentarily. He came down at half-past eleven, broke the undercarriage of his machine, but escaped injury himself. From Joyce Green, Lieutenant R. S. Tipton ascended soon after eight. He saw no airships and at half-past nine was compelled to land owing to engine trouble. Thereupon, Captain L. da C. Penn-Gaskell rose, but after half an hour he, too, was forced to land with a failing engine. Then Tipton went up again. Although this time he reached 9,000 feet and remained in the air for nearly an hour, he saw nothing but the flashes of anti-aircraft guns. He landed safely twenty minutes after eleven. A naval aviator from Whitley Bay rose to guard Newcastle, but no airships came his way.

The raid demonstrated that numerous well-lighted landing grounds were absolutely essential for the effective employment of aeroplanes at night, so that they could leave the vicinity of their aerodromes to hunt the enemy some distance away. Finally, the absolute necessity of a plentiful supply of search-lights was emphasised. Without their aid it is impossible for aviators to find the hostile airship which, if lit up by searchlights can be seen several miles off.

The Germans started the 1916 campaign with a very serious attack, but not on London. The improved defences had had their effect and London was not attacked again until the beginning of April.

The air raid of the 31st January, 1916, was undoubtedly a belated effort to attain Liverpool, which project had been abandoned in the preceding fall. It marked the occasion on which German airships penetrated to the farthest westerly point in England ever reached by them, and was the most ambitious effort which the naval service had as yet attempted, the entire available squadron of new airships being employed.

Since the last raid and during the intervening three and a half months, something had been done towards rendering navigation over this country somewhat more difficult in that the new lighting restriction orders were then in process of enforcement. Nevertheless, the area which was attacked by the airships was still virtually defenceless, so that the raid was carried out under the most favourable circumstances from the enemy's point of view.

Nine airships crossed the North Sea—L.11, L.13, L.14, L.15, L.16, L.17, L.19, L.20 and L.21— these representing the whole force of naval ships of the new standardized type then available. They appeared off our coast in successive groups, the first group, L.13 and L.21, arriving shortly before 4.50 p.m. off the Norfolk coast, while L.11 and L.20 which had the whole length of the Wash to traverse, did not come over the land till 7.10 p.m. The weather conditions while rendering the voyage of the airships easy and safe considerably affected their movements. The mist and fog on the coast disturbed their calculations at the outset, confusing their ideas of landfall, and throwing their direction inland considerably out of the line intended. The landfall of the airships was evidently planned to take place between the Inner Dowsing and Haisboro' light-vessels in a south-west direction, course being changed to W.N.W. and N.W. on sighting the south-east corner of the Wash. These courses if persisted in, and opening out fanwise from the coast, would have brought the airships over the Liverpool—Manchester—Sheffield district, passing over that of Burton, Derby and Nottingham. The fact that the German Admiralty officially reported that the airships had visited the Liverpool—Man chester district tends to show that this was the planned objective.

The ship which penetrated farthest inland was the L.14 (Kapitanleutnant Böcker). She crossed the coast at Holkham Bay soon after six o'clock and steered to King's Lynn. After passing to the north of Peterborough she made a course for Birmingham, well north of which she passed on her westward journey which extended to Shrewsbury, the farthest point reached, at about ten o'clock. She then turned, followed an erratic path to the north of the Wash, visiting on her way Ashby-de-la-Zouch, Derby, Ilkeston, Nottingham, Newark, and finally out to sea slightly north of Skegness at about two o'clock in the morning, having been over England for some eight hours. But this was exceeded by the ill-fated

L.19 (Kapitanleutnant Loewe) which during the eleven hours she was overland traversed a path somewhat south of that of the L.14, extending beyond Kidderminster to Bewdley, where she passed over at half-past ten. She made her way back to Winterton by a tortuous path, touching on the way the outskirts of Birmingham, Coventry, Rugby Kettering, Kimbolton, the most southerly point reached in the area of the operations, Huntingdon, Stoke Ferry and Norwich. Von Buttlar in his L.11, after striking the most perfect entry via the Wash, correctly turned north-west in accordance with the plan, but passing a little too well to north he reached East Retford just before ten o'clock. After a tortuous journey he went out at the mouth of the Humber at midnight. He was overland for nearly five hours and gained the farthest north at Scunthorpe, where he attempted to bomb the Frodingham iron and steel works, but his missiles fell on the Redbourne iron works, curiously enough in darkness, in contrast to the former works, which, having received no warning were in full blast. Two men were killed there, and the engine and boiler-house was slightly damaged.

Mathy, in his L.13, exhibited his usual prowess. Entering at 4.50 p.m. south of Cromer he arrived at East Dereham, then made for King's Lynn, then Grantham, Long Eaton, Derby, then to Stoke-upon-Trent and Newcastle-under-Lyme, which he reached at about half-past eight. Had he continued he would most probably have arrived at the objective—Liverpool—but he turned about, bore south past Stafford, then swung round to Burton-upon-Trent, continued towards Macclesfield, rounded Buxton and made out to sea due east, his point of exit being above Skegness in close proximity to that of Böcker in the L.14.

The L.21 (Kapitanleutnant Dietrich II) entered with Mathy and steered a course which did not deviate to any great extent from Mathy's until Derby had been passed. Here Dietrich turned to the south, passed Stafford, Wolverhampton, Dudley, Tipton, Walsall, east to Nuneaton, Market Harborough, Kettering, Ely, Thetford, and so out to sea slightly south of Lowestoft at about half-past eleven, while Mathy was by Skegness. Of the others L.20 (Kapitanleutnant Stabbert) entered the Wash, got as far as Burton-upon-Trent and more or less retraced her steps and out to sea between Wells and Cromer. L.16 (Oberleutnant Peterson) merely skirted Norfolk and similarly L.17 (Kapitanleutnant Ehrlich), but much nearer the coast. Breithaupt in the L.15 traversed Norfolk and Lincoln, but never got very far from the Wash.

Burton-upon-Trent was bombed by no less than three ships, and there is little doubt that bright lighting may be held largely responsible for its fate. A small fire started by the first bomb of the leading airship may have contributed to attract further missiles from her successors. It is undoubtedly the case that the variation in the lighting of the different towns must have rendered the navigation of the airships very difficult. In all, 205 high explosive and 174 incendiary bombs were dropped, the casualties from which were 70 killed and 113 injured.

Over and around London there was thick ground mist. Of the sixteen pilots who had gone up from stations in the vicinity of the capital three were injured, two, unfortunately, so seriously that they subsequently died. They were Majors L. da C. Penn-Gaskell and E. F. Unwin; both highly experienced officers whom we could ill-afford to lose. Penn-Gaskell was in charge of the training squadron at Northolt. When warning came through for aeroplanes to go up, if weather permitted, Penn-Gaskell gave instructions for nobody to leave the ground until he himself had had a " chukker round " in the fog to ascertain if the conditions were such as to warrant him sending up the pilots in his charge. In a very heavy ground mist he took off at a quarter to seven. Scarcely had he left the aerodrome when he was observed to crash. His machine had struck a tree on the outskirts of the aerodrome. He received severe injuries to which he succumbed five days later. Unwin went up from Joyce Green at about a quarter to eight and like Penn-Gaskell, blinded by the mist, he crashed into a tree almost at once. He died from his injuries two months later, on the 23rd March. The Royal Flying Corps suffered irreparable losses when these two gallant and highly-efficient officers died in the performance of duties which they considered too dangerous to delegate to their juniors.

There was a chase of a phantom airship that night. Flight Sub-Lieutenant J. E. Morgan, who went up from Rochford at about a quarter to nine, was at 5,000 feet when, according to his report, he saw a little above his own level and slightly ahead to starboard, " a row of what appeared to be lighted windows which looked something like a railway carriage with the blinds drawn." Morgan thought that he had sighted a hostile airship only some 100 feet away, so he fired at it with his Webley Scott pistol, whereupon he says that " the lights alongside rose rapidly " and disappeared. Heading west he fired a Very light in the hope that he might be near an aerodrome, but he got no answering signal. He next discerned a " blur of yellowish light," which he thought might be Southend pier. On coming down, however, he discovered that what he had seen were the lights of a large Dutch steamer off Thames Haven. Flying round it he asked with his electric torch for his bearings, but the only answer he got was from the guns and searchlights of the Thames Haven defences. Morgan, knowing that these indicated " land or ships at sea " decided to descend. From the reflected light of one of the searchlight beams he made out a coastline to which he steered and came down into a " muddy water course." He was uninjured. With the help of some Royal Engineers he was able to extricate his undamaged machine from the mud, and thirty-six hours later he was able to fly his machine back to Rochford where he arrived on the afternoon of 2nd February. Four machines from Yarmouth and two from Castle Bromwich searched the mists in vain.

The raiders did not all get back safely. It would appear that the L.19's flight had been too protracted and that she had not enough petrol to carry her home. Her engines were rendered partially useless, and it was not till three p.m. that she reached the neighbourhood of Borkum. Here she broke down entirely and drifted away to the westward. At 7.30 a.m. on the 2nd February she was sighted water-logged ninety-five miles east by north of Spurn by the skipper of the trawler *King Stephen*, who although offered money by the airship commander to take him and his crew on board refused to do so as he feared that the airship crew, if he took them on board his boat, would take charge and carry him off to Germany. He therefore returned to the Humber with his report and the airship shortly afterwards sank, all on board perishing.

CHAPTER VII

THE STRAFING OF SCOTLAND

IT was during 1916 that Germany attempted to reap the harvest of many years of patient and persistent endeavour. She had achieved a type of craft which no other nation either possessed or could build. With her rigid airships she had been preeminent in peace and their tryout in war was not unpromising. She had learned that for successful results from air bombing continuous and unremitting attacks must be kept up. She had also learned with some chagrin that even improvised defences had a limiting if not crippling effect on the boldest of raiders. Could she but succeed in rapidly breaking the morale of the British nation anything would be worth while. What is the loss of a few airships and their precious crews if a war of nations is to be won? This was Germany's temper when she launched in the spring of 1916 a sequence of raids with hammer-blow regularity, which were to reduce England to a state of prostration and impotence with no breathing space for recovery or for the perfecting of counter weapons, if indeed any such did exist. If here and there some sort of respectable defences were encountered many places existed where the defences were insignificant. If London could not easily be reached the whole heart of Britain lay open to be attacked at leisure. So Germany thought. But she must act quickly. She knew that given time there is always a counter weapon to any innovation, and once the element of surprise passes new weapons cease to be effective.

If the defences of London were being stiffened up, the north still presented easy game, and so before noon of the 5th March three airships, L.11, L.13 and L.14, left their sheds for a raid on England. The leading airship, L.13, crossed the Lincolnshire coast shortly after 9 p.m. and made inland, probably looking for Sheffield and the industrial district of south-west Yorkshire. Failing to find her objective and not attempting to beat back against the rising north-east wind, she made a remarkable course at high speed across England, passed out at Deal, having dodged a naval machine from Eastchurch in the snow, and avoided the fate of the L.19 by landing in Belgium. The second ship, L.11, came in over the coast of Holderness and followed L.13 as far as Lincoln. There she turned and got back to the Humber, bombed Hull at about one in the morning and then went out to sea at the Spurn. The third airship, L.14, came in at Flamborough Head and after a period of doubt as to her whereabouts found Hull and bombed it shortly after midnight, afterwards going out to sea at Tunstall.

Snow began falling at Hull shortly before nine o'clock, and in the intervals when it ceased the town was bombed at leisure. The casualties suffered were very severe, seventeen persons being killed and fifty-two injured as a result of the thirty-three bombs dropped on the town. The damage was to houses, shops, a café, a public house, almshouses, etc. The military damage was confined to a dockshed and crane.

On the 31st March, 1916, five naval airships left their north German sheds and steered for England. The tactical plan in the main appears to have been an attack against the munition factories in eastern England; the area attacked was that lying east of a line from Woolwich to Cromer. Mathy, in the L.13, on this occasion came in at Saxmundham and penetrated no farther than Stowmarket, which, however, he bombed. When over the objective he was hit by a tracer shell. A copy of a message written by Mathy himself and intended to be sent by wireless was picked up near Stowmarket next morning. It had evidently been blown overboard. It ran:

"Chief of the Naval Staff, High Seas Fleet, 10 p.m. Have bombarded battery near Stowmarket with success. Am hit; have turned back. Will land at Hage about 4 a.m.—L.13."

L.16 (Oberleutnant Peterson) came in at Winterton soon after ten o'clock and reached Bury St. Edmunds close on midnight. Here Peterson dropped his load of bombs, turned, and went out to sea by Lowestoft.

Böcker, in the L.14, described a most unusual course. Passing inland from the Would lightship soon after eight o'clock he bore down south, reaching as far as Brentwood in Essex. He there turned about after being fired at by the Kelvedon Hatch gun. He went back north, reached the Colne Valley, and changing his mind came back again, passed Chelmsford, and when he was between Brentwood and Billericay he swerved to the mouth of the Thames; continuing the turn he passed north again, this time via the mouth of the Blackwater, Colchester, Ipswich and out to sea by Saxmundham. His bombs had been dropped on Sudbury, Braintree, Blackmore, Doddinghurst, Springfield, Stanford-le-Hope and Thames Haven.

Next, Breithaupt, in the L.15. He was the first to arrive and crossed the coast at Dunwich at a quarter to eight. He steered a course which brought him to the eastern outskirts of London. He got as far as the Thames at Rainham. Here he was heavily assailed by guns at Purfleet, Abbey Wood, Erith, Erith Marsh, Southern Outfall, Plumstead Common and Plumstead Marsh, and was lit up by numerous searchlights. Attempting to elude the bombardment, Breithaupt turned northwards, hurriedly jettisoned his bombs on Rainham, but to no avail, as shrapnel from the Purfleet guns which struck his ship made a large rent in her side. He now determined to get away with all speed, so he sought the coast, avoiding the Thamesmouth defences. When L.15 was east of Brentwood, shortly before ten o'clock, Second Lieutenant A. de B. Brandon in a B.E.2c, who had risen from Hainault farm, overtook the airship and climbing above her dropped explosive darts without apparent result. The airship could no longer rise owing to loss of gas. Brandon then boldly passed along her side in order to get behind, but was greeted with heavy machine-gun fire from the crew. After an unsuccessful attempt to drop an incendiary bomb and more darts on the ship, Brandon lost sight of his quarry and returned to his aerodrome. The airship headed due east and throwing out all possible ballast circled twice over Foulness as though undecided to risk leaving land, but eventually made out to sea. Her injuries were fatal, and she finally broke her back and fell into the sea from a height of 2,000 feet at the Knock Deep at eleven o'clock. The crew were rescued by two trawlers at about midnight, one man being drowned. An unavailing attempt was made to tow the airship in, but she foundered off Westgate.

Dietrich I, in the L.22, made the northern feint and spent his time and fury on Cleethorpes at the mouth of the Humber. Six high explosive bombs were dropped there and a chapel used as a billet by the 3rd Manchesters was completely destroyed, twenty-nine men being killed and fifty-three wounded.

On going out to sea he was attacked by anti-aircraft guns firing from a paddle mine-sweeper in the Humber, but without result.

A military ship was suspected as taking part in this raid, but only appears to have made a timid incursion to Ipswich, hurriedly retreating after being fired at by a pom-pom. Another military vessel is supposed to have approached Suffolk, but to have turned back before reaching the coast.

It is remarkable that telephonic and telegraphic communication to the naval air stations at Cranwell, Yarmouth and Felixstowe broke down that night at the critical time, particularly as all but one of the raiders made their landfalls in the vicinity of Yarmouth and Felixstowe and the northernmost not very far from Cranwell. In all, eight naval and nine military airmen went up. In addition to Brandon, Second Lieutenant C. A. Ridley from Joyce Green pursued and attacked the L.15, but without success. Lieutenant J. W. Bailey who had ascended from Northolt in a B.E.2c, crashed soon after rising. He was dead when picked up.

Next a raid was carried out the following night by two naval airships. Soon after eleven o'clock on the night of the 1st April, L.11 came in by Seaham and after dropping some bombs on villages reached Sunderland, on which fourteen high explosive and seven incendiary bombs fell. Considerable damage was done mainly to shops and dwelling houses; 22 persons were killed and 128 injured.

She then coasted south to Middlesbrough, where two high explosive bombs were dropped on vacant land. Thence she passed seawards to Skinningrove, and before leaving the coast dropped two more high explosive bombs there which, however, did no damage. The L.17 was off Flamborough Head for about an hour dropping bombs in the sea. Either on account of engine trouble or her commander's lack of energy, she never came inland. Both raiders were sought but not found by four naval machines from stations in the vicinity of the Tyne and the Tees.

Scotland next came within the radius of action of the German raiders and L.14 and L.22 accordingly set out for the journey on the 2nd of April, 1916. Dead reckoning brought Böcker and Dietrich I above and below St. Abb's Head; Böcker in the L.14 came up the Firth of Forth and struck Leith and Edinburgh at midnight. He then retired. Dietrich I, in the L.22, first went inland north of Berwick-upon-Tweed and had some bomb practice at Lamberton and Chirnside. He passed out again at his original landfall at a quarter to ten, and then also made up the Firth of Forth, keeping closer to the coast than Böcker had done. He flew round Edinburgh, while Böcker was over the city, dropping bombs here and there and then passed down the Firth and so away. Peterson, in the L.16, was out that night and penetrated a short way into Northumberland near Blyth. He may have had Newcastle as his objective, but he did not get far enough south. His bombs wrought very little damage, but he scored a hit on the aerodrome at Cramlington, where some woodwork was burnt.

While the naval airships were raiding Scotland and Northumberland, two military airships crossing from Belgium made a raid on the east coast. One came in at Orfordness at half-past eleven, flew to Wickham Market, then turned to Ipswich and finally out again whence she had come, unloading the bulk of her bombs, nearly all incendiary, in the vicinity of Ramsholt and Alderton, and breaking a few windows. The other came in at the mouth of the Blackwater at eleven o'clock, and after passing over Witham and Chelmsford reached Waltham Abbey about midnight. Here she was heavily engaged by the Waltham guns and replied by dropping all her bombs (twenty-five high explosive and sixty-five incendiary). No casualties were inflicted and only a few houses were damaged. She went back on a course slightly north to that of her entry and passed out to sea at Clacton at one in the morning.

In Scotland, naval seaplanes went up from East Fortune and Dundee; in the north of England two military aeroplanes went up from Cramlington and saw nothing. One caught fire on landing and was blown to pieces by its own bombs, the pilot miraculously escaping unhurt. In East Anglia machines to the number of seven went up from Hounslow, Croydon, Sutton's farm and Hainault farm, but although an airship was sighted it could not be overhauled, and three machines were damaged on landing.

As a reminder that the campaign was not off, a single naval ship passed over the north-eastern corner of Norfolk in the early hours of the 4th April. Bombs were dropped, but neither casualties nor damage ensued. A second ship was believed to have attempted to come over, but nothing was seen of it. Although several naval ships had been reported in the North Sea on the 4th April, none came to raid that night. Two ships came again on the next night. One penetrated Durham as far as Bishop Auckland; the other bombed the eastern outskirts of Hull, and then went to Skinningrove, which was also bombed to some effect. In Durham one child was killed and five persons injured and many humble cottages were wrecked. At Hull four persons were injured and some glass broken. At Skinningrove, however, the laboratory of the ironworks was wrecked. Military aeroplanes went up from Beverley, Scarborough and Cramlington, but failed to locate the airship. Lieutenant J. Nichol who went up in a B.E.2c from the last station crashed into a house and was killed.

The effect of the loss of the L.15 on the night of the 31st March is clearly seen in the anti-climax of the four succeeding raids.

CHAPTER VIII

THE SECOND RAID ON SCOTLAND

ALTHOUGH the easiest way open to a bold enemy to menace our insular security was by air, the dangers of invasion by land could by no means be ruled out. Further, hostile naval attacks on various coastal regions, although hazardous were possible operations for which our navy had to be continually prepared. When at the beginning of 1916 information came to hand that the Germans were collecting large numbers of lighters and barges at bases in Flanders the danger could not be overlooked, and the Admiralty undertook that if an attempt at invasion was to be made it should fail. Measures for meeting such eventualities had long been worked out and the Admiralty proceeded to make their dispositions accordingly.

On the afternoon of the 24th April, 1916, news was received that a rebellion had broken out in Ireland and the German High Seas Fleet appeared to be moving, and there was reason to believe that the Germans intended to support the insurgents by a demonstration against the east coast of England. We apprehended that under cover of a sortie by the High Seas Fleet a force might be detached to raid our bases at Yarmouth or Lowestoft or even the Thames estuary. The expected attack materialised.

On the morning of the 24th April eight Zeppelins, L.9, L.11, L.13, L.16, L.17, L.20, L.21 and L.23 left the north coast of Germany to co-operate with the German High Seas Fleet. The airships were accompanied by the two older vessels, the L.6 and L.7, which, however, returned home next day after coming some of the way over the North Sea. Late that evening the airships made the East Anglian coast, but only six of them crossed inland; one made for Lincolnshire, four for Norfolk and one for Suffolk. It is fairly clear that these airships had come to reconnoitre for the German naval detachment which was making for Lowestoft and Yarmouth. Admiral Scheer has explained that this demonstration was calculated to force the British fleet out of port and that he expected to achieve this by bombarding coastal towns and carrying out air raids on England the night the fleet was out. The weather that day was not favourable for air raiding and it is doubtful whether the airships would have come over if the naval operation had not demanded an accompanying aerial demonstration. The airships appeared to be so wholly bound up with the naval operation that land objectives were quite secondary. They avoided searchlights, evaded defending aeroplanes and made off as soon as fired on. The bombs thrown caused no casualties, save one woman who died of shock and one man injured. The damage done was insignificant.

To complete the picture the army carried out an airship raid the following night (25th April). Five ships came over, but one turned back without reaching the coast, and another, after dropping bombs on the steamer *Argus* in Deal harbour was turned back by the guns at Walmer. Of those which raided, one attacked Kent with little effect; another bombed Harwich, to little better purpose, under fire from all the local anti-aircraft guns. The third, the L.Z.97 (Hauptmann Linnarz) made the boldest attempt. She entered the mouth of the Blackwater and got to Seven Kings, where guns and aeroplanes turned her sharply about for home.

One of the officers on board the airship has described this raid in *The German Air Force in the Great War* by Major Neumann (Eng. trans., pp. 118 *et seq.*). He says:

" At high speed we steer for their city, the Commander standing ready on the bombing platform. The electric lamps which he has switched on glow with a dull vari-coloured light. His hand is on the buttons and levers. ' Let go!' he cries. The first bomb has fallen on London! We lean over the side. What a cursed long time it takes between release and impact while the bomb travels those thousands of feet! We fear that it has proved a dud—until the explosion reassures us. Already we have frightened them; away goes the second, an incendiary bomb. . . . At the same time on come the search-lights reaching after us like gigantic spiders' legs; right, left and all around. In a moment the bright body of the ship lies in the beams. . . . It is difficult to understand how we manage to survive the storm of shell and shrapnel, for according to the chrono-meter we have spent a good hour under furious fire. When London lies far behind us we can still recognise it distinctly; the searchlights still stabbing the dark-ness—more than sixty of them looking for the bird that had already flown. Silence closes in around us and everything beneath seems stricken with death."

The bombs which Lampel thought were dropped on London actually fell in a line between Fyfield and Ongar and others on Barkingside. Dealing with his reception when nearing the coast on the outward journey Lampel says:

"Then hell is let loose! They have long lain in wait for us down below there and now the little dot of a gondola light has betrayed us. In a moment the searchlights of the warships of the Thames estuary have caught us and hold us fast. Again a withering blast of fire is directed against us. Put out that light! The Commander reaches over the steersman's shoulder and switches it off. But the ship once caught cannot get away from the search-lights. Shell after shell shrieks up at us, among them incendiary shells; they burst dangerously near. After ten minutes the light grows fainter and the firing dies away."

A very important feature of this raid was the performance of the defending aeroplanes. Three rose from Hounslow, three from Sutton's farm and two from Hainault farm. Lieutenant W. Leefe Robinson from Sutton's farm got near enough to the airship to fire at her with a machine-gun when she was over Seven Kings; but flying at 8,000 feet he was still some 2,000 feet below her and his fire proved ineffective. Captain A. T. Harris from Hounslow also got to within 2,000 feet of the airship, but his Lewis gun jammed and the airship eluded the searchlights and disappeared eastwards. In addition a machine was up from Dover on patrol to the North Foreland. Two machines crashed on landing, but no pilots were injured.

The following night (26th April) a single military airship visited Kent, but only came a little way inland, being over the coast for some twenty minutes hidden in the thick mist from an aeroplane up from Westgate. Her bombs fell in the sea off Deal.

It was now forcibly brought home to the Germans that London was becoming more and more difficult of approach. The attack of the L.15 against Woolwich on 31st March had been turned by guns, and the ship never got a chance of rising or dropping her bombs before being hit; again a military ship which came to Waltham and Enfield on the 2nd April succeeded in dropping her bombs, but was nevertheless turned back by the guns, while the attack of the 25th April was likewise frustrated. So that even that part of London which appeared to be the weakest—midway between Woolwich and Waltham—was also getting out of reach, to say nothing of the rising tide of the aeroplanes. The threat to Woolwich had been met. When the order "Concentrate on Woolwich" went forth, guns, lights and telephones were quickly installed on the 31st March, just in time to meet the attack there the very same night. After Woolwich, Waltham. Again we were just ready though not completely so. The gun which was mounted on the 2nd April was the weapon which that same night turned the raider away from the explosive factories.

The spring airship offensive was brought to a close on the 2nd May by nine airships, eight naval and one military. The attack extended from north of the Wash in the south to south of Cromarty in the north. It will be recalled that the coast between these limits was considered by us to permit of a possible landing in force, but the raid may not have had this object in view, although it certainly appeared to be very largely naval in scope. The movements and apparent courses of the airships would seem to point to an intention of carrying out a reconnaissance of our naval patrols in Scottish waters before coming overland. The plan appears to have been as follows: One ship, the new military L.Z.98, was to attack the Humber or the east Midlands, another, the southernmost naval ship was directed to raid the Yorkshire industrial district. The remaining seven ships were ordered to move on Scotland with a view to reconnoitring and bombing the naval bases of the Forth, possibly the Tay and certainly Cromarty. It is conceivable that an attack on the Clyde was also in view. With the possible exception of L.21 which bombed York, and certainly that of L.20 which made for Cromarty, none of the raiders exhibited any clear purpose of attacking any definite objective after they had reached the coast, although it may be presumed that L.14 was searching for Rosyth and that L.11 had the same object in view, but was put off by her encounter off the coast with H.M. Ships *Portia* and *Semiramis*. The Skinningrove iron works were bombed twice, it is true, but the two attacks were rendered brief and ineffective owing to the surprise of a newly-established anti-aircraft gun at this point which may have scored a hit on one of the raiders, whilst overland all ships with the exception of L.20 showed indecision in their movements. They threw their bombs vaguely at such lights as they may have taken to indicate towns or ironworks. Two, if not three, of the ships that were deflected to the north Yorkshire coast threw at least thirty-nine high explosive bombs at a mass of burning heather on Danby moor which had been set on fire by a single incendiary bomb dropped at a venture by a previous raider nearly an hour before. The brand new military ship tried her wings round the mouth of the Humber, but did not raid. Yorkshire suffered the only casualties; nine persons were killed and thirty injured. The damage was comparatively small. A hospital and several houses were wrecked.

In so far as Scotland was concerned, only two of the raiders actually crossed the coast. Böcker, in the L.14, crossed the mouth of the Firth of Forth, after touching Eyemouth on the southern side, and came in by Arbroath. He may have been looking for Rosyth, but low rain clouds and a rising south-east wind may have upset his plans. He seems to have mistaken the north bank of the Tay for that of Forth. He hugged the coast from Arbroath to Fife Ness and thence out to sea. His bombs fell in fields, injuring a horse and breaking a pane of glass. Kapitanleutnant Stabbert, in the L.20, made a remarkable course. He entered Forfarshire at Lunan Bay just before ten o'clock and made straight for Loch Ness, evidently bound for Cromarty. Realising that with the changing weather conditions rendering all landmarks invisible, his objective could not be attained, he turned about over the Caledonian canal and steered in a more or less easterly direction, going out to sea south of Peterhead. His stay in Scotland extended over four and a half hours. His journey to the Caledonian canal had brought him almost to the extreme limit of his radius of action.

H

Cromarty is some six hundred miles distant from Cuxhaven, and so extended a raid could only have been accomplished in favourable weather. In the event the strong south-easterly wind which he encountered on his homeward journey put his base out of reach, so he made for the nearest land. At ten in the morning on the 3rd May, flying very low, he struck the coast of Norway south of Stavanger. Some of the crew, including the second in command, saved themselves by jumping into the water before the land was reached, but the rest stuck to the ship which drove on over the land and crashed into a hill, the Jaataaberg, near Sandnaes. Rising in a terribly damaged condition she fell into the Hafrsfjord, where she broke in two.

Stabbert dropped bombs on Craig Castle, which, being beyond the restricted lighting area was lit up, and suffered a little damage in consequence. Others he dropped in fields. No casualties were inflicted by either of the Scottish raiders.

Eight machines went up, but failed to see anything of the airships. Captain J. H. Herring's gallant action that night is worthy of mention. He was then serving with No. 15 Reserve Squadron at Doncaster. On hearing bombs exploding in the distance, he asked to be allowed to take the air, notwithstanding the fact that " no order to take action had been received." Having obtained permission, Herring rose at eleven o'clock and searched the skies for over an hour, but owing to profuse

Zeppelin L.20 wrecked in the Hafrsfjord, Norway, after raiding Scotland on the night of the 2nd May, 1916

To face p. 100

clouds he saw no hostile aircraft. He landed at Bramham moor soon after midnight. When at three in the morning no " resume normal conditions " order had come through, Herring once again went up, " hoping to cut off any hostile aircraft which might have lost their way." He passed through several layers of clouds, but again saw no airships. Finally he returned to his aerodrome at Doncaster and landed at about five o'clock.

CHAPTER IX

THE AIR DEFENCE GROWS

THE Zeppelin was approaching its zenith. The instrument had well-nigh reached the limit of war development, and if it could not now accomplish the purpose for which it had been nursed and fostered, it never would. Since the beginning of the war it had grown twice as big and twice as powerful. While the L.3 and L.4 which first attacked England in January, 1915, were of some 800,000 cubic feet capacity, with a speed of some forty-five miles an hour, the Zeppelins now coming forward were double this size, and in speed could exceed sixty miles an hour. The ceiling, that is to say the greatest height attainable, had risen from eight to thirteen thousand feet, while the load and calibre of the bombs had increased accordingly.

The airship was eminently adapted for long reconnaissance, as it could remain in the air for days, which no aeroplane could do. It could carry a very great load and could hover over its objective to make its aim more certain. But the hydrogen which gave it support and height was at once its strength and its weakness. Mixed with air, hydrogen forms a most inflammable mixture and this rendered the airship liable to spontaneous combustion, as when L.10 was struck by lightning at Neuwerk off Cuxhaven on the 3rd September, 1915, or when the L.18 caught fire at Tondern while being inflated in its shed on the 17th November, 1915. However, the British navy was determined to cripple Zeppelin activity, certainly in so far as it provided the German navy with means of observation. Frequent sallies into the Heligoland Bight were carried out by combined naval and air forces with the object of enticing Zeppelins out, in order to cut them off from the mainland and destroy them, and concurrently to attack the sheds. The attempts of 1915 had not proved unfruitful, the Zeppelins frequently rising to the bait, but our seaplanes proved incapable of the task. They occasionally even failed to rise from the water. Those were the days when a light swell was sufficient to waterlog the best seaplanes of the time and losses were common. An important lesson, however, was learnt from these attempts, particularly that which took place on the 24th March, 1916. It was then found that although the primary object—the raid on the Tondern sheds—failed, it nevertheless roused the enemy sufficiently to draw a considerable portion of the High Seas Fleet out of harbour. So that at the next attempt the bombing of the Zeppelin sheds was an incident on a larger plan.

On the 4th May, 1916, all available squadrons of the Battle Fleet, accompanied by the seaplane-

carriers *Vindex*, *Engadine*, and *Campania*, set out
to attack the enemy airship sheds at Tondern, so
as to draw out the German fleet and to entice it
over previously laid minefields and there bring it
to action. Eleven Sopwith " Baby " seaplanes took
part. Owing to various failures, only one actually
attacked. The pilot dropped two 65-lb. bombs on
Tondern, but through the mist could not discern
where the bombs had fallen. A Zeppelin, the L.7,
came out and approached the British fleet. At the
third round from a 6-inch gun of H.M.S. *Galatea*,
firing at 12,000 yards range, the airship was hit
and after breaking her back fell blazing headlong
into the sea. Seven survivors were rescued and
taken prisoner by the submarine E.31, which also
completed the destruction of the wreck. The plan
to draw out the German fleet failed, but the minefields were successfully laid.

Following the destruction of L.7 no further raid
on England took place until the end of July. The
Germans were no doubt awaiting the delivery of
the newer Zeppelins in which the ceiling particularly
had been greatly increased. Meanwhile, home
defence measures grew apace. When Sir John
French was brought home from France at the end
of 1915 to fill the newly-created post of Commander-
in-Chief, Home Forces, the army was ready to take
back the responsibility for aerial home defence,
which had for so long been in the hands of the navy.
The date of the actual transfer for London was the

16th February, 1916, and by April the responsibility embraced the whole of the United Kingdom.

Such experience as was available made it clear that the power of navigation and the radius of action of Zeppelins rendered London liable to attack from any direction. Any effective defence, therefore, was necessarily one which encircled the metropolis. As far as guns were concerned, the scheme employed was one in which they were disposed at supporting intervals over an area including London, and as large a zone round it as the number of guns available permitted, so that an attacking airship would be illuminated and under fire for a considerable time before reaching its objective as well as while over the objective, should she reach it. The scheme originally provided for eighty-three guns for the defence of London proper, but this was never reached owing to lack of guns, and the number actually employed did not exceed sixty-four. Outside the gun perimeter advanced lights were disposed for the purpose of illuminating the enemy before he came within range of the guns, so as to enable our aeroplanes to see him and attack, and the guns to open fire the moment the enemy came within range.

On the re-transfer, Colonel M. St. L. Simon, an engineer officer, was brought home from France to take over the anti-aircraft gun defences of London. Sir Percy Scott had already formed a ring of gun stations to cover the central portion of Greater London, bounded roughly by lines joining Kenton,

Mill Hill, Finchley, Wanstead, Blackwall, Honor Oak, Somerstown, Kingston, Richmond and back to Kenton. The centre of the ring was covered by the guns sited in Regent's park, Tower bridge, Battersea, etc., and the searchlights were somewhat highly concentrated in the centre of London. To Colonel Simon also passed the plans for the future which embraced an area bounded by Hoddeston, Epping, Hainault, North Ockenden, Southfleet, Crockenhill, Purley, Windsor, Mill Hill, Potter's Bar, Tyler's Causeway, Essendon and back again to Hoddeston. In the area there were to be seven control centres, and outside it a single ring of about forty miles diameter of lights to work with the aeroplanes. The controls and lights were to be connected by telephone to the headquarters of the Home Forces. Guns and lights he found had been sited independently of one another. The guns in situ were a miscellaneous collection—pom-poms, six pounders, French 75-mm. guns on pit mountings, 4-inch guns, 4.7-inch guns, 3-inch 5 cwt. guns, a 3-inch 19 cwt. gun and a few 3-inch 20 cwt. guns, including a " solid " one.

With regard to aerial defence, twenty machines, which had already been dispersed two apiece at ten stations, were placed on the 1st February, 1916, under the control of a single officer—Major T. C. R. Higgins—who was in command of the newly-formed No. 19 Reserve Squadron at Hounslow. Soon after, the various Royal Flying Corps stations round

London and all London defence detachments were grouped into the newly-formed 18th Wing on the 25th March, 1916. This wing was placed under the command of Lieutenant-Colonel F. V. Holt, who had been specially brought home from France for the purpose.

So far, home defence was carried out through the existing organisation for training purposes, but experience had already shown that although home defence was bound up with training, in order to grapple with the problem effectively it was necessary to have operational units for home defence distinct from training units. The intermingling of training and home defence machines on the same aerodrome under the command of the training squadron commanders involved mutual interference and both training and home defence suffered accordingly. The logical conclusion was the formation of squadrons specifically for home defence; the first to be so formed was No. 39, which was to gain such distinction in extinguishing the airship as a weapon of offence. This redoubtable squadron came into being with headquarters at Hounslow on the 15th April, 1916, and was formed from the various close detachments for the defence of London; Major T. C. R. Higgins was its pioneer commanding officer. For a beginning, the small number of aeroplanes available only allowed of this one squadron to be allotted for the immediate protection of London, and the only two flights of the squadron were disposed at Sutton's farm and Hainault farm respectively, being controlled from headquarters at Hounslow. The underlying principle was to concentrate the machines on the ground and distribute them in the air. No. 39 Squadron was to be the nucleus of a very considerable organisation, but this took some time to develop. The great advance, however, had been made.

By the end of June four more defence squadrons were in being, namely No. 33, at Bramham moor and Knavesmire, No. 36 at Cramlington, No. 50 at Dover, and No. 51 at Norwich. A special home defence wing was formed on the 25th June, 1916, which became merely the Home Defence Wing, dropping its number—16—at the end of July. On its formation this wing not only included the five home defence squadrons in being but also five more that were contemplated, namely Nos. 37, 38, 75, 76 and 77. Colonel Holt, who had so well organised the aeroplanes for home defence, was fittingly placed in charge of the wing. Home defence now had a properly organised and trained air force. It was the recognition that in modern warfare such a force had become a necessary combatant factor if the industries and population of a belligerent were to be protected from assault from the air.

One result of the concentration of home defence machines at particular stations was that in the event of a raid no machines went up from a training aerodrome unless a defence flight was also stationed there. This led to a certain unpopularity with the public of the Royal Flying Corps detachments at training stations. People noticed machines at certain aerodromes flying about during the day but inactive during a raid the same night. Nevertheless the separation of home defence from training led to beneficial results. The training squadrons being relieved from home defence work were able to turn out more pilots, and the home defence pilots became more specialised for their particular work, being specially trained in night flying. The aeroplane adopted was the B.E.2c with the 90 H.P. Raf engine. The chief reason for its choice was its inherent stability. Although considerable controversy ranged round this type of machine not only for home defence but for use in the field, in the long run it more than justified itself, as practically all the successes by aeroplanes against airships were achieved with this machine.

Effective night flying was only possible with careful organisation. Before the war frequent landings in the dark had been made, and the experience gained was embodied in the Royal Flying Corps training manual of 1914. On the aerodrome four flares were arranged in the form of an L, the landing being effected down the longer arm with the short arm to the front. The most suitable flare recommended was a bucket containing half a gallon of petrol. This was found to burn for half an hour and was visible from a distance of eight miles on a clear night. Obstacles on the aerodrome were marked by red lights. The first task Major Higgins set himself was to standardise night flying equipment and the armament of the attacking aeroplanes. The petrol flares were wasteful. So a flare burning paraffin was devised called the "Money" flare. Asbestos was packed in a wire cage and dipped in a bucket of paraffin. It consumed about one and a quarter gallons an hour and its light penetrated mist and fog. The Money flare proved efficient, simple and economical and was in use long after the air raids had ceased to trouble us. Many landing grounds were sited, some for normal use and others for emergency. They were divided into three categories, first, second, and third class, each distinguished by the number of its flares. A barrage line was laid down, including aerodromes at distances varying from ten to thirty miles apart and stretching from Dover to Edinburgh. Home defence squadrons were split up into three detached flights with headquarters at some central point. The scheme was that a flight should be concentrated on a small aerodrome and patrol towards the aerodrome of the nearest adjoining flight. Thirty of such aerodromes were in working order by the winter of 1916. Searchlight companies were allotted to home defence squadrons and these aeroplane lights, as they were called, were trained to work in close co-operation with the aeroplanes, distinct from the gun lights. The field of operations of the Home Defence Wing extended to the Wash. The squadrons north of the Wash

B.E.2c Aeroplane with 90 h.p. Raf Engine

Aeroplanes of this type were extensively used in combating raiding Zeppelins. Five German airships were shot down over Great Britain by pilots flying these machines

[*To face p.* 110

worked through the appropriate garrison commander
—the Humber, the Tees, the Tyne and Edinburgh.

So far the miscellaneous collection of guns had
been retained, but in June, 1916, Colonel Simon put
forward a scheme in which a ring of gun stations,
each comprising two 3-inch 20-cwt. guns, was to be
formed round the thickly populated parts of London,
the interior being filled by single gun stations.   The
underlying idea was that hostile raiders should be
met at the edge of their objective by heavy bursts
of shell-fire and so be turned back.   Outside the gun
circle a double line of searchlights was proposed
over and around which the defending aeroplanes
could manœuvre.   The scheme was approved and
the abolition of the heterogeneous collection of unsuitable guns soon followed.

Around London, along the coast, and throughout
the length of Great Britain, lines of observer posts
were established.   Information as to the course of
hostile craft was transmitted by telephone to various
control centres, which in turn were in direct communication with the Horse Guards.   This information was sifted in the "Operations Room," and the
civil population warned accordingly.   The defences
were now becoming more and more organised and
more and more effective.   If the main onslaught was
still to come we were getting ready to meet it.

CHAPTER X

THE GREAT AIRSHIP OFFENSIVE OF 1916

THE German great airship offensive was launched at the end of July, 1916, some three months after the last raid. This quiescent interlude was not altogether unexpected, as the nights towards the middle of the summer were neither sufficiently long nor dark enough to favour raiders, and a similar break had occurred during 1915. There may have been other reasons for this inaction. The airships may have been held in reserve for the coming naval activity which culminated in the Battle of Jutland at the end of May. Again, the German air force was fully pre-occupied on the western front and was suffering the severest trials it was ever called upon to undergo, and this affected both its heart and strength, for it was at the battle of the Somme, in 1916, that the British air force attained its greatest mastery over the German air service—a mastery which was never attained or surpassed by any belligerent later. Further, the enemy may have been waiting for the improved airships—the L.30 class —which were just coming forward. Four attacks followed in fairly rapid succession, the first on the

28th July and the fourth on the 8th August; after which there was a pause of over a fortnight before the attacks were resumed.

The raid of the 28th July, 1916, was feeble and ineffective. Of ten naval airships which set out only six raided, and of these only one—the L.13—penetrated any distance inland. This ship came in south of the Humber, at North Somercoates, half an hour after midnight, and steered as if making for Nottingham. When slightly to the east of Lincoln, bombs were dropped which broke a few windows at Fiskerton. She continued as far as Newark and then turned. After dropping bombs at villages to south-east of that place and breaking a few more windows, she made out to sea at Boston at half-past two in the morning. Little need be said of the others: L.17 and L.24 flew about and above the Humber. Bombs were dropped on Killingholme and Immingham without any result whatever. A calf, however, was killed at East Halton. L.16 bombed the neighbourhood of Hunstanton and L.11 that of Cromer, also to no purpose beyond killing a cow. L.31, scarcely a fortnight off the stocks, flew round Lowestoft and did not trouble to drop bombs overland. Fog and mist had frustrated the raid more effectively than our defences might have done.

On Zeppelins being reported in the vicinity of Wells-next-the-Sea on the night of the 30th July, aeroplanes rose from Killingholme, Holt, Bacton, Yarmouth, Covehithe and Felixstowe. No raid materialised, but at 5.15 a.m. on the 31st, the Cove-hithe machine, a B.E.2C piloted by Flight Sub-Lieutenant J. C. Northrop, met and engaged an enemy airship thirty miles out at sea; a trivial acci-dent, however, made him break off the combat and the airship got away. The following night (31st July), ten naval airships again approached to attack. Two turned back and of the remaining eight, one, L.16, raided Lincolnshire and penetrated to Newark. Bombs were dropped all along her route; of casualties and damage, however, there were none. Another looked at Thanet and left behind a few broken windows. The others sprawled all over Norfolk and Suffolk and even over a part of Cambridgeshire. The profit and loss account of the raid showed casualties nil; a few shattered windows; and one horse and two bullocks injured, for the expenditure of fifty-six high explosive and forty-four incendiary bombs. All the airships showed impatience and hurry. They got as high as they could and flew as fast as they could. Many aeroplanes were up during the raid, but saw nothing through the mist.

Next, on the afternoon of the 2nd August, six naval Zeppelins left their sheds and flew westwards over the North Sea bent on a raid. They all crossed our coasts. Four spent their time over Norfolk and the north-east corner of Suffolk; one raided the neighbourhood north of Harwich, while the L.31 cruised off Thanet as she had done two days pre-viously. L.21, which penetrated farthest inland, crossed the coast at Wells-next-the-Sea and bore south to Thetford aerodrome, by whose flares she was attracted. Five bombs were dropped here shortly before one in the morning, but did no damage whatever. The airship then turned to the east and made for the sea, dropping four bombs at Covehithe as she passed out and eight more in the water. Three other ships all covered paths more or less inside the area swept out by the L.21. There were no casualties from these ships, although some horses were killed, some injured, and a little damage was done to property, mostly broken windows. The L.11 which raided the Harwich district was heavily engaged by guns, but seems to have limped home, probably hit. Her bombs slightly injured a boy at Kirton, where also some cottages were damaged. L.31, the newest ship, crossed Deal at one in the morning, but on being picked up by searchlights and fired at by guns she left the land and followed the outline of the coast until she was just due east of Dover, where she was driven off and away by accurate gunfire. None of her bombs fell on land. Many machines rose that night. A few naval pilots got within striking range of airships, but their efforts were unsuccessful.

On the night of the 8th August, nine airships out of eleven starters appeared at various points between the Wash and the Tweed. Norfolk, the East and North Ridings of Yorkshire, Durham, Northumberland, and Roxburghshire were all involved. Hull,

I

however, which was bombed by the L.24 was the only place to suffer to any extent, ten persons being killed and eleven injured. Material damage was confined to a few houses and shops. The only other casualties of the raid were inflicted by the L.11, which dropped bombs on the small watering place at Whitley Bay. One man, one woman and three children were injured as the result of thirteen bombs dropped there, and in addition some houses were damaged. The L.30 tried to destroy the works at Skinningrove and at Seaton Carew, but without any success whatever. Thick mist prevailed all over England that night. Only one machine rose. Flight Lieutenant B. P. H. de Roeper went up in a B.E.2c from Redcar shortly after midnight. When at 6,000 feet he saw the bursts of bombs at South Bank. He was proceeding in that direction when he observed bombs bursting on his aerodrome to his rear. He then turned to follow in the wake of the bursts. Arrived at the coast by Saltburn he discerned an airship, held in a searchlight beam. He was then at some 8,000 feet and the airship some 2,000 feet higher. Despite all his efforts to close —he even dropped his bombs into the sea to gain height—he was unable to reach the airship. Nevertheless, he pursued her twenty miles out to sea until he lost her in the mist. He landed at Redcar just before three in the morning.

These four raids were all conspicuous for the timidity displayed by the airship commanders, and not without reason. The gun defences were proving formidable all along the line—cushy places to bomb were becoming rarer and rarer, but far more sinister was the danger from the aeroplanes. They were beginning to swarm whenever Zeppelins attempted a footing, and further, the instruments at their command were becoming more and more deadly.

The Zeppelin menaced England; its spawn, the Drachen kite balloon, was an unwelcome spectator of our doings on the western front. Both these craft had a common vulnerability in their hydrogen, and anxious thought was being brought to bear on the problem how best to take advantage of it.

Experience in aerial fighting in France had proved that the most effective weapon was the machine-gun. It followed that the machine-gun should be tried against Zeppelins. If the airships should fail to ignite, the riddling of the gas bags might cause such leakage that the airships might be forced to descend. But this was found to be quite unreliable. The great need both for Zeppelins at home and kite balloons abroad was for a bullet which would not only pierce the gasbag but also ignite the gas. So attention was concentrated on the incendiary bullet. Warneford in his first attack on a Zeppelin on the 17th May, 1915, had used incendiary or " flaming bullets " as they were called. Although he believed the Zeppelin had been hit, the gas failed to ignite, and this gave rise to the unfounded supposition that the ballonets of Zeppelins were surrounded by inert gas. Later experience proved that incendiary bullets might pass through the envelope without setting the gas alight, and special explosive bullets were accordingly devised. These, if they hit the framework of the airship and detonated, almost invariably ignited the hydrogen. Improved explosive bullets were brought out in the spring of 1916 for use against Zeppelins over England, while for attack of kite balloons in France an incendiary bomb, composed mainly of phosphorous, had been produced. For the same purpose the French were using a form of incendiary projectile called the Le Prieur rocket, in addition to light incendiary bombs. When the Royal Flying Corps were charged with the duty of destroying enemy kite balloons on the eve of the battle of the Somme, in 1916, attacks were delivered along the whole British front by means of Le Prieur rockets and phosphorous bombs. In two days, 25th and 26th June, 1916, nine balloons fell to the attacks of our airmen, seven by the rockets and two by the bombs. The rockets proved superior to the bombs. They were fired at short range from an attachment to the struts of the attacking aeroplane, and their success led to their adoption for anti-Zeppelin purposes at home. However, they saw little service in England, as they were soon superseded by the more accurate and deadly explosive ammunition.

At the beginning of 1916 the armament provided for anti-Zeppelin work consisted of twenty pound high explosive and sixteen pound incendiary bombs. Shortly afterwards a form of explosive dart was brought out by Commander Ranken, R.N., and these were also issued to the defending machines. Apart from the difficulties of effective aim from above, these missiles were no less dangerous to the population than the Zeppelin bombs themselves. Finally, when suitable explosive bullets became available the counter weapon for the Zeppelin was at hand. A form of tracer bullet which merely assisted ranging was early employed by both the Germans and ourselves in aircraft. But when an incendiary bullet was produced we were very averse to using it in the field. After a very thorough investigation, combined tracer and incendiary ammunition was taken into use in the field just before the battle of the Somme opened in 1916 for employment in aerial combat. This ammunition was found particularly effective against kite balloons.

During Flight Sub-Lieutenant Northrop's encounter with a Zeppelin in the early morning of the 31st July, he had fired two trays of explosive and tracer bullets and was in process of firing the third, when the tray came away from the Lewis gun and hit him in the face, in consequence of which he was forced to break off the combat. Again, during the raid of the 2nd August, Flight Lieutenant C. T. Freeman who had risen in a Bristol Scout from the seaplane-carrier *Vindex*, managed to get above a Zeppelin and straddle her with Ranken darts.

Although the pilot reported that some of the darts got home, apparently they did not damage the airship to any extent. After the attack he flew to rejoin his ship, but his engine failed and he came down into the sea, and after some hours in the water was picked up by a Dutch vessel and taken to Holland. His Zeppelin experience, however, was to have a very important sequel as we shall see later. Other pilots had also engaged Zeppelins with explosive and tracer ammunition, and the airship commanders now had become aware of their danger. All that was required was a definite tryout in which the new ammunition should find its mark, and so prove its capabilities. The time was near at hand.

After a lull of nearly a fortnight, a solitary military airship crossed from Belgium on the night of the 23rd August, and although she dropped thirty-four bombs, all the damage done was slight injury to a barn at Trimlee near Felixstowe. She was not seen and was unmolested. The military airship service was certainly at a low ebb. It was soon to disappear entirely. The following night (24th August) the naval service attempted a big demonstration. Twelve airships started out to raid, but in the event only four crossed the coast. The most important feature of the raid was the dash by a single ship to London, the first to penetrate its defences since the 13th October, 1915. L.31 indeed made up for her previous failure. She came in along the Thames estuary, passed Canvey Island and made for Barking.

She then turned south, crossed the Thames at
Millwall, made a sweep round Woolwich, crossed
the Thames again, and went out overland by Shoeburyness. Her bombs were dropped at Millwall,
Deptford, Greenwich, Blackheath, Eltham and Plumstead at about half-past one in the morning. These
killed nine persons and injured forty others. As
might be expected, considerable damage was done to
property in these crowded areas. One house was
completely destroyed by a 2-cwt. bomb which fell
upon its roof, nothing being left of it but the outline
of its foundations. Of the other three, one was off
Dover and came a little overland at Folkestone, but
dropped her bombs at sea; a second rounded the
Naze, but was driven off by the guns. Her bombs
were dropped in the Oakley area, narrowly missing
the explosive works there. Beyond a wrecked cow-
house there was little damage. The third came in
at Aldeburgh and dropped bombs between Wood
bridge and Ipswich at about midnight. She broke
some telegraph wires and glass.

At one point the airship could not be found, owing
to her keeping above the clouds. A searchlight was
kept searching along a break towards Ipswich, so
that, should she attempt to cross this break, she
would come into the beam. After repeatedly
manœuvring to cross the clear patch the airship made
straight for the searchlight and tried to put it out
with bombs. She failed and then made off.

Eight naval and seven military aeroplanes were

up that night.   Several pilots sighted Zeppelins, but only one, Captain J. W. Woodhouse, of No. 50 Squadron at Dover, actually attacked.   He left the ground at a quarter past two and almost immediately sighted the L.32 held in the Dover searchlights. He pursued her over the Channel but got into some clouds.   On emerging he again sighted the airship, and manœuvring underneath, fired into her.   He was then at 7,000 feet and estimated the airship to be some 2,000 feet above him.   While reloading he lost sight of his target for good.   Being now uncertain of his bearings he flew around and finally picked up the Dover searchlights, which guided him home.

CHAPTER XI

LEEFE ROBINSON'S RAID

GERMANY'S inmost spleen was stirred. The greatest and most numerous airship fleet the world had ever seen was mobilised for the climax for which two years of patient experiment had prepared the way. Who will ever know what great expectation went forth with this armada? Even if the German army on the western front had come near to being shattered by the British troops on the Somme, and even also if the German air service had been reduced to impotence by the Royal Flying Corps, the German nation may have hoped that by a sudden and gigantic onslaught on the heart of Great Britain they would not only retrieve their fortunes but might well achieve the victory which now appeared unattainable by other means. The culminating point of the Zeppelin had been reached, and if it could not now accomplish its purpose, all hope of its ever doing so would have to be abandoned. Success in war is largely dependent on surprise, and in so far as surprise was lacking in this project it proved an unutterable failure. Not only were those charged with our defences not surprised, but they had perfected their instruments and were actually awaiting the opportunity to try them out against just such an effort as the enemy put forward, and the result was for the enemy one of the greatest débâcles on record. With one fell swoop the airship was virtually eliminated as a military weapon, and the fall of 1916 will always be memorable in the annals of British history.

The great raid matured on the 2nd September, 1916. Every available naval airship was told off for the attack, and in addition army airships were detailed to co-operate. In all sixteen started, twelve naval and four military, and all but two, one naval and one military, crossed the coast. The naval ships were L.11, L.13, L.14, L.16, L.17, L.21, L.22 L.23, L.24, L.30, L.32 and S.L.8; L.17, however, turned back off the coast of Norfolk. Of the military ships only one was definitely identified—the S.L.11; of the four which set out one turned back at the Long Sand lightship. The raid followed the usual naval tactics—a swoop on London by the main body from the Norfolk coast with a simultaneous demonstration by an odd ship or two to the north, in this case the Humber district. One ship, the wooden Schutte Lanz S.L.11, reached London but never returned. She came unheralded from Belgium and appeared over the Foulness sands at twenty minutes to eleven. She steered in a north-westerly direction and was at Coggeshall shortly after eleven. Soon after she turned west, and at midnight she described a small circle near Great Chesterford but proceeded on her westerly course to Royston, where she picked up the Great Northern railway line which she followed to Hitchin. She then carried on to Luton and began to approach London from the north-west. Her sighting bombs were dropped at London Colney, but did no damage. Others soon followed with no better result. When the airship was due north of London, she turned towards the capital, and just before two in the morning was south of Alexandra Palace. Here she came under heavy fire from the Finsbury park gun and was picked up by the Finsbury park and Victoria park searchlights. Turning to the north-east over Tottenham, well caught in the searchlights, she came under heavy fire from other guns of the London defences. Retreating north she now dropped most of her bombs, but no casualties were inflicted and little damage was done.

Of the many airmen who had ascended to the attack Lieutenant W. Leefe Robinson, of No. 39 Squadron, went up from Sutton's farm shortly after eleven o'clock with instructions to patrol between his aerodrome and that at Joyce Green. He climbed in his B.E.2c to 10,000 feet. Although the night was clear he saw nothing for two hours, but at ten minutes past one he observed an airship caught by two searchlights to the south-east of Woolwich. Being now at some 13,000 feet he made in the direction of the illuminated Zeppelin, hoping to cut her off on her way eastward. He slowly gained on her, and judging her to be only some 800 feet below him, he decided to sacrifice speed in order to maintain height. Unfortunately she passed into some clouds, and Leefe Robinson lost sight of her and could not find her again although he searched for fifteen minutes. He then resumed his patrol. At ten minutes to two he noticed a red glow in the north-east of London. Believing this to be an outbreak of fire he made towards it, and at five minutes past two he again saw an airship held in the beams of searchlights. This time he was determined not to lose his quarry, so he sacrificed height and made full speed, nose-down, towards the airship. In spite of the heavy anti-aircraft fire he drew close up. In his report he says:

"I flew about 800 feet below it from bow to stern and distributed one drum along it (alternate New Brock and Pomeroy). It seemed to have no effect; I therefore moved to one side and gave it another drum distributed along its side—without apparent effect. I then got behind it (by this time I was very close—500 feet or less below) and concentrated one drum on one part (underneath rear). I was then at a height of 11,500 feet when attacking Zeppelin. I hardly finished the drum before I saw the part fired at glow. In a few seconds the whole rear part was blazing. When the third drum was fired there were no searchlights on the Zeppelin and no anti-

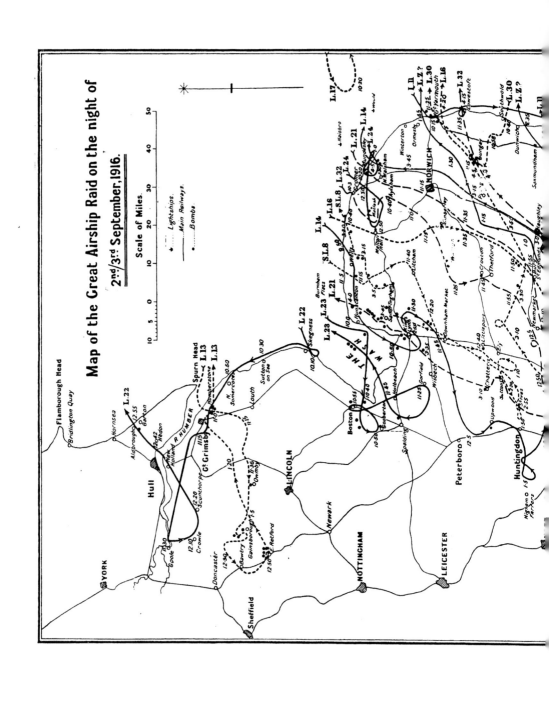

Map of the Great Airship Raid on the night of 2nd/3rd September, 1916.

Scale of Miles.

10 0 5 10 20 30 40 50

Lightships. ------
Main Railways. ————
Bombs. ••••••••

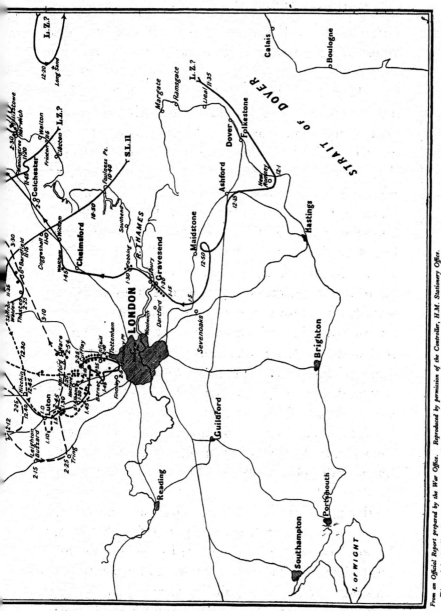

From an Official Report prepared by the War Office. Reproduced by permission of the Controller, H.M. Stationery Office.

This map depicts the raid on England with the greatest airship fleet ever assembled. Sixteen vessels took part, and all but two crossed the English coast. The raid might well have proved most disastrous but for Lieutenant Leefe Robinson's epic feat in shooting down the S.L.11 over Cuffley. It marked the first occasion on which an airship was shot down by machine-gun fire from an aeroplane, and the effect on the raiders was devastating. It killed the most ambitious airship raid of the war and marked the decline of the airship menace at the same time. The immediate effect of Leefe Robinson's achievement was the hurried retreat of the fleet, with the result that for an expenditure of over sixteen tons of bombs only four people were killed and twelve others injured. The damage done was insignificant.

The German Air Raids on Great Britain, 1914-1918.   Captain Joseph Morris.   Sampson Low.

aircraft was firing. I quickly got out of the way of the falling, blazing Zeppelin and, being very excited, fired off a few red Very lights and dropped a parachute flare. Having very little oil and petrol left, I returned to Sutton's farm, landing at 2.45 a.m. On landing I found I had shot away the machine-gun wire guard, the rear part of the centre section, and had pierced the rear main spar several times."

The S.L.11 fell flaming headlong to earth at the village of Cuffley. Being a wooden ship she burned for nearly two hours after she reached the ground. All the bodies of the crew were completely charred and all objects on board more or less destroyed by fire. The effect on her consorts was enormous, and the most gigantic air raid of all time simply fizzled out. Further, it was an ill-omen; it was the beginning of the end of the airship menace.

The L.16 had made a bold attempt to reach the capital from the same direction as that of the S.L.11, but when at St. Albans she witnessed the hurricane of shell with which the Schutte Lanz was being assailed, lost heart, wavered and turned, hurriedly dropped her bombs at Essendon, and fled as far from London as possible before even the aeroplanes had come into action. Her commander must have seen an intense illumination suddenly appear. He flew away and to safety at about sixty miles an hour. The L.32 was at Tring when the S.L.11 flamed up. Her commander then turned abruptly off to the east. He went slowly for a while, probably considering the situation and apparently determined to make for home after having dropped such bombs as he had left as near London as he dare approach. They dropped at Hertford and Ware. He then made off full speed for Lowestoft and so out to sea and sanctuary. The paths of the London raiders were gradually contracting. L.21 was at Flitwick and passed east to Hitchin, where her commander saw the glare of the burning S.L.11. So he, too, at once turned homewards at high speed, shedding his bombs by the way as he went. L.14 at the time of the catastrophe was at Thaxted. Like the others, her commander swung his ship sharply round for home, dropped his bombs willy-nilly, and put his ship through a performance test. The naval Schutte Lanz—the S.L.8—had reached St. Ives when her commander apparently saw the glare in the sky fifty miles away. Instinctively knowing what this signified he tore back at high speed to the coast, dropping his bombs here and there. L.30 did not penetrate to any extent. She flew inland a bit near Lowestoft and was well away before the raid had really started. L.24 made a timid incursion near Cromer, dropped bombs to no purpose and left the troubled atmosphere at Bacton. The L.11 coasted between Great Yarmouth and Harwich and dropped bombs at both places, but only two fell on land and those at Yarmouth. No more was heard of her that night. The L.23 raced about the Wash at high speed between eleven and twelve o'clock and dropped bombs in a most arbitrary fashion.

Of the northern raiders, L.22 turned away from the Wash and on approaching the Humber turned inland towards Goole which she reached at half-past eleven. She then turned, crossed the Humber and made out to sea south of Hornsea, having dropped her only bombs in open fields in the parish of Flinton north-east of Hull. L.13 may have been intended for Sheffield. She entered at the mouth of the Humber, dropped a few bombs here and there and turning by Bawtry she bore down on East Retford, which town she bombed severely. Three gasometers were hit, ignited and destroyed. She then made back to the mouth of the Humber and away.

Remained two military ships. One crossed the coast at Littlestone at midnight. Her route touched Ashford, Maidstone, Sevenoaks. Then she passed to Gravesend, where, on being fired at by the Dartford guns, she dropped most of her bombs. Crossing the Thames she was taken on by the Tilbury and Fobbing guns shortly before half-past one. Again she dropped bombs and putting on full speed followed the great Eastern railway past Chelmsford, Colchester, Ipswich and out to sea at Saxmundham. This was evidently the airship which Leefe Robinson had seen shortly after one. She was then being held by the Hartley and Southfleet searchlights shortly before dropping her first bombs. The other military ship came in at Frinton about eleven o'clock. At about half-past eleven, when at Mistley, south-east of Manningtree, she throttled down and lowered an observation car. For some reason unknown the supporting cable broke. The car with about five thousand feet of wire attached was found next morning at Mistley. After the accident the airship commander appeared to continue on a course which would have brought him round to the north of London, but when over Wixoe at half-past twelve he gave up the idea, turned sharply about and ridding himself of his bombs, made direct for Great Yarmouth, shedding the winch of the lost car on the way.

This raid is outstanding for many reasons. It demonstrated in the most definite manner that the most effective defence against raiding airships was a carefully worked-out scheme in which guns, lights and aeroplanes each had a definite rôle; and in which each supported the others and all were absolutely necessary. Further, that the aeroplanes could only play their part usefully when the airships were held in searchlight beams. It marked the first occasion on which an airship was shot down in the air by machine-gun fire from an aeroplane. Leefe Robinson's heroism in achieving this great event was recognised by the grant of the Victoria Cross. When the thing had once been done it could and would be done again; in fact, it would become common, but the pioneer effort of Leefe Robinson stands out like a beacon. No event in the history of the air attacks by German airships on Great Britain had such a complete and overwhelming effect on the German airship service as the shooting down in flames of the wooden Schutte Lanz. The moral effect on the population was immense. The catastrophe was witnessed by millions, and the awful conflagration was visible for over fifty miles. When it is considered that this was the greatest effort of its kind ever put forth, that the bombs were in number and weight the maximum ever dropped in one raid, and that the casualties and damage were insignificant, the immediate effect of Leefe Robinson's achievement is small compared with its broader effect on the airship campaign, as we shall see. In all, 261 high explosive and 202 incendiary bombs, of a total weight of sixteen tons, were counted. The casualties were four killed and twelve injured. The damage was hardly noticeable.

The flights carried out on this memorable night by the defending aeroplanes are worth recording. They illustrate the methodical plan which had been evolved for the hunting down of the Zeppelins. No. 39 Squadron came in for the lion's share as their patrols were athwart the normal paths of approach to London from the north-east. The squadron at this time had been brought up to strength. When formed, the headquarters was located at Hounslow and the first two flights stationed, one at Hainault farm and one at Sutton's farm. In

K

August the headquarters was transferred to Wood-
ford in Essex and a third flight was established at
North Weald Bassett. To meet the raiders of the
2nd September, each flight sent up single machines
at a two hours' interval, the patrols being so arranged
that the line North Weald Bassett, Hainault farm,
Sutton's farm, Joyce Green and Farningham was
continually watched. The first machines were sent
up at about eleven o'clock. Lieutenant Leefe
Robinson from Sutton's farm was to patrol the
line Sutton's farm—Joyce Green; Second Lieutenant
C. S. Ross from North Weald Bassett, the line North
Weald—Hainault; and Second Lieutenant A. de B.
Brandon from Hainault farm, the line Hainault—
Sutton's farm. For the second patrol which
ascended at about one o'clock, Second Lieutenant F.
Sowrey from Sutton's farm was to watch the line
Joyce Green—Farningham; Second Lieutenant J. I.
Mackay from North Weald Bassett, the line North
Weald—Joyce Green; and Second Lieutenant B. H.
Hunt from Hainault farm, the line Joyce Green—
Farningham. Ross was up for two hours and then
was compelled to land, crashing his machine in
doing so. Brandon returned to Hainault at about
half-past one with nothing special to report. Sowrey
came down with engine trouble after about a quarter
of an hour. Mackay reached 10,000 feet, and when
at the Joyce Green end of his patrol observed the
S.L.11 held in a searchlight to the north of London
and gave chase. When he was within a mile of her

he saw her fall in flames. Leefe Robinson had already got her. Returning to Joyce Green he saw another airship north-east of Hainault, but after a fifteen minutes' chase he lost sight of her and resumed his patrol. He eventually landed at North Weald after four in the morning. Hunt, when 10,000 feet up, saw an airship lit up by a searchlight and some 800 feet above him. He climbed to attack but as he was about to close, the airship—the S.L.11—had just been ignited by Leefe Robinson. In the blaze of light he saw the L.16 only a short distance away. He at once pursued her, but dazzled by the glare he lost sight of her just as she passed out of the area illuminated by the burning ship. Hunt now lost his bearings but continued to patrol, and half an hour later, about three in the morning, he saw a third airship, this time about 2,000 feet above him. Although he made an attempt to get even with her he lost her and finally landed at Hainault farm at about a quarter to four.

At Dover, No. 50 Squadron sent up three machines at about half-past eleven. Captain J. W. Woodhouse patrolled for two hours between Dover and the North Foreland. He saw no airship and landed at Manston. Lieutenant H. A. M. Fraser was also up for two hours in the vicinity of Dover, but saw nothing of the raid. The third, Captain J. Sowrey, was compelled to return almost immediately owing to engine trouble. While all this activity in the south, No. 33 Squadron at Beverley in the north sent up Captain R. C. L. Holme at about one o'clock, but he crashed on getting off.

Naval machines were also busy in their night watches of the coast. Flight Commander A. R. Arnold rose in a Henri Farman from the Isle of Grain at about half-past one. At two o'clock he sighted an airship dropping bombs and being shelled over London. He accordingly steered in that direction, but lost sight of his quarry, and after climbing to 13,000 feet, and still being unable to discover the airship, he attempted to land on observing the Chelmsford aerodrome flares in the distance. While coming down he saw the S.L.11 fall in flames. Unfortunately, owing to a ground mist he crashed in landing and was slightly injured. Flight Lieutenant E. Cadbury went up from Yarmouth shortly after ten. At about eleven o'clock he sighted a hostile airship which had been picked up by the Lowestoft searchlights, but he lost her in the clouds and he landed just before midnight. From Covehithe rose Flight Sub-Lieutenant S. Kemball. He was up from just before ten to just after eleven, but saw no airships. Flight Sub-Lieutenant E. L. Pulling ascended at midnight from Bacton to look for hostile airships which had been reported. After a flight of some three-quarters of an hour he landed, having failed to see anything of the raiders, but immediately afterwards he went up again and stayed up for over an hour, reporting on his return that he had seen incendiary bombs burning to the south-

east of the aerodrome.   After another short pause
he rose again, and after a further flight of an hour
and a quarter's duration he landed at a quarter-past
four in the morning, having this time seen nothing.
In addition to these three flights that night, Pulling
had also been up for a local flight in the early evening
before the raid.   This was the stuff the Zeppelins
were up against.

The machine with which Leefe Robinson achieved
his success was the B.E.2c.   Indeed, every machine
up that night with the exception of Arnold's Henri
Farman was a B.E.

CHAPTER XII

THE FALL OF THE THIRTIES

It was not to be expected that the destruction of the military Schutte Lanz S.L.11, in the small hours of the 3rd September, would deter the Germans from attempting any further attacks on the city. The naval raiders would be the more eager to demonstrate to their military colleagues the greater efficiency of the naval service. So on the 23rd September, eleven naval airships came out to show their superior prowess. Of the eleven, viz. L.13, L.14, L.16, L.17, L.21, L.22, L.23, L.24, L.31, L.32 and L.33, one, the L.16, turned back when half-way over; another did likewise, but appears to have overcome her trouble and returned to the fray. The three newest and best ships were to attack London, as they were the only vessels which had the ghost of a chance of reaching the capital. The main body this time seems to have been ordered to keep north of the Wash and to attack the area between there and the Humber. The L.21 might possibly have been earmarked to follow in the wake of the " thirties," but either by accident or design she contented herself with Stowmarket, a favourite alternative objective for timid raiders. As for the L.23, she made a most half-hearted attack upon the Norfolk coast. She never came overland and loosed bombs in the sea by Cromer and Overstrand.

For the German raiders things were going from bad to worse. The L.32 and L.33, the triumph of Zeppelin skill and the pride of the German navy, were to be lost in one night and, most hateful of all, to fall to the British defences; and were it not for Mathy the L.31 would also have stayed west that night, but her end was not yet. The plan of attack on London that night clearly shows the respect and fear which the airship commanders now entertained for the formidable northern defences of London. The lesson of the S.L.11 had been learnt. On this occasion, instead of following the well-trodden route via Norfolk, two "thirties" made the attempt from the south, entering by Dungeness and giving the defenders of the city a wide berth. The very newest ship, the L.33, may have been intended to accompany these, or alternatively she may have been detailed to detract the attention of the defences from L.31 and L.32. Actually she came by the Crouch and faced the formidable hurricane in the north-east.

Mathy's effort in the L.31 was masterly, so much so that he surprised the vigilants and got away with it, the only one of the trio to do so. At about eleven he was near Rye; half an hour later he was at Tunbridge Wells. Continuing through Surrey he arrived at Kenley about half-past twelve, where he dropped four high explosive bombs which damaged a few houses. By dropping flares he blanketed such searchlights as pierced the darkness to light him up, and he cut across London from south to north—Mitcham, Streatham, Brixton, Kennington being bombed by the way. He then flew across the Thames, and when over Lea Bridge road began to jettison his remaining bombs. These inflicted severe casualties in residential quarters, twenty-two persons were killed and seventy-five injured, while damage was confined to dwelling-houses. He had crossed from Streatham to Walthamstow almost without being fired upon. Either the mist concealed him or the attention of the defences was fixed on the east and not on the south; the fact remains that he crossed London almost unmolested. Leaving shortly before one he got safely away, going out by Great Yarmouth. Peterson in the L.32 came in with Mathy at Dungeness. He at once dropped six of his bombs on his landfall, causing insignificant damage. He then went inland for a time and turned round. When almost at sea again he appears to have overcome his trouble and so returned to the assault, having spent an hour near his landfall. He was at Tunbridge Wells about a quarter-past twelve. A little later he dropped seven bombs on a search-light which had opened on his airship.

Dropping bombs here and there he crossed the Thames by Dartford at one in the morning. The mist on the south side of the river rendered the airship difficult to see and so shielded her from action by the defences there. North of the Thames he was engaged by guns and searchlights, which he attempted to bomb. Having relieved himself of his missiles he now bethought himself of home, but he was seen by an officer of the Royal Flying Corps, who was also in the air. Second Lieutenant F. Sowrey, who was patrolling from Joyce Green to Sutton's farm, found the L.32 ten minutes after one and immediately attacked. In his report Sowrey says :

"At 12.45 a.m. I noticed an enemy airship in an easterly direction. I at once made in this direction and manœuvred into a position underneath. The airship was well lighted by searchlights, but there was not a sign of any gunfire. I could distinctly see the propellers revolving, and the airship was manœuvring to avoid the searchlight beams. I fired at it. The first two drums of ammunition had apparently no effect, but the third one caused the envelope to catch on fire in several places; in the centre and front. All firing was traversing fire along the envelope. The drums were loaded with a mixture of Brock, Pomeroy and tracer ammunition. I watched the burning airship strike the ground and then proceeded to find my flares."

L.32 began to fall slowly, finally crashing to the ground in flames at Snail's Hall farm, Great Burstead, south of Billericay. All on board perished with her. The wreckage burned for nearly an hour. Second Lieutenant Brandon, who saw the combat from his aeroplane some distance away, says in reference to Sowrey's projectiles that the airship looked as if she were " being housed with a stream of fire."

Böcker in the L.33 separated from Mathy and Peterson off the Goodwins, and crossing the estuary of the Thames, made his landfall at the Foulness sands at about a quarter to eleven. He made for the Crouch which he followed to its source, passed Billericay and was over Wanstead at about midnight. He had already dropped bombs by the way, but his main load was carefully preserved. He then turned and came over West Ham where gun after gun and light after light got on to his ship. Turning again he began to drop his bombs, variously 50 to 300 kilogrammes, on Bromley-by-Bow and on Bow itself. These inflicted eleven fatal casualties and injuries to twenty-five people. The damage done was considerable, many factories, business establishments and houses being wrecked. The airship now finding the fire to which she was being subjected dangerous to her safety, and having probably been seriously hit, climbed as best she could and went off in a north-easterly direction. At about half-past twelve, when approaching Chelmsford, she was attacked by Brandon who was up on patrol between Hainault and Sutton's farm. Brandon hung on to her for twenty minutes, firing at every available opportunity, but although he saw his shots bursting all along her body the airship did not catch fire. After this combat, his ship rapidly losing gas and height, Böcker began to jettison everything possible overboard. He went out to sea at West Mersea at a quarter-past one, but realising the hopelessness of his plight he came back and brought his ship to earth in a field between Little Wigborough and Peldon. There she took fire, but owing to the great loss of gas she was not badly burnt. Böcker and his crew survived and were captured, having first presented us with a shop-soiled specimen of the latest product of Friedrich-shafen. If Brandon's bullets did not bring about the L.33's fall, the glory of the gunners is enhanced by his gallant attempt.

With regard to the five Zeppelins which went north, the only outstanding feature was a fell attack on Nottingham by the L.17. Between midnight and one o'clock she dropped eight high explosive and eleven incendiary bombs on the unhappy city. For the whole raid we counted 202 high explosive and 166 incendiary bombs dropped. The casualties totalled forty killed and 130 injured. These, together with the damage done, were suffered mainly by London and Nottingham. The mists in the valley of the Lea and in the valley of the Trent shielded the attacking airships. At Nottingham the L.17 was not even seen. Otherwise our casualties might have been less and our bag the greater.

This raid, following on Leefe Robinson's achievement, proved beyond doubt the great value of the aeroplane in the scheme of defence. The patrol line, North Weald Bassett—Hainault farm—Sutton's farm—Joyce Green—Farningham, was fast becoming a sure aerial shield for London. When at half-past eleven Böcker was reported approaching the capital, No. 39 Squadron sent up three machines on a three-hour patrol of this line. When an hour later Mathy and Peterson were announced, two more machines were ordered up. At Dover, too, No. 50 Squadron sent up machines, as also did No. 51 Squadron at Thetford; from the latter station Second Lieutenant M. H. Thunder crashed while taking off and was killed. To meet the northern onslaught one machine rose from No. 33 Squadron at Beverley. Eleven naval pilots went up from stations at Westgate, Eastchurch, Covehithe, Yarmouth, Bacton and Cranwell. Zeppelins were attacked in two cases, without result, off Yarmouth.

Scarcely two days had elapsed to mourn the loss of the L.32 and L.33, when eight naval ships left their sheds to raid England on the 25th September. One turned back and two others failed to come overland, confining their operations to manoeuvres off the coast of Norfolk. London and its environs for

The remains of Zeppelins L.32 and L.33 after the raid on the night of the 23rd September, 1916.

Top.—The L.33 after compulsory landing at Little Wigborough, Essex.

Bottom.—The wreckage of the L.32 after being shot down by an aeroplane over Billericay, Essex

To face p. 142

miles round was left severely alone. The main
attack was delivered by four ships on Yorkshire,
Lancashire and Lincolnshire, while Mathy in his
L.31 struck new ground with a south coast tour to
the Isle of Wight and Portsmouth. Two or more
military airships were seen or reported in the Straits
of Dover and off the Belgian coast in the early
morning of the 26th; only one came overland and
this merely encircled Pevensey Castle and then returned to Belgium whence she had come. Mathy
navigated his L.31 with skill, and made in succession the three headlands, Dungeness, Beachy Head
and Selsey Bill. He then crossed to Sandown in
the Isle of Wight, being seen over that place at
about half-past eleven. Turning north, he passed
over Ryde, crossed Spithead and made straight for
the entrance to Portsmouth harbour. Here his ship
was picked up by searchlights and all anti-aircraft
guns were ranged on her, but Mathy, flying at a
great height, passed on over the forest of Bere, and,
turning east, went by Midhurst, Cuckfield, Lewes,
Hailsham and so out to sea at St. Leonards. He
came overland again near Rye and went out to sea
for good at Dungeness, where he had made his first
landfall. On his homeward journey at half-past two
in the morning, when off Dover, he dropped three
bombs in the sea. These were the only bombs we
heard or saw. It is difficult to account for his
failure to attack Portsmouth harbour or the dockyard. Possibly his mission may have been one

of reconnaissance only, as at that time there was intense activity by German submarines in the Channel.

Two ships can be dismissed at once. One was observed about thirty miles out to sea off the coast of Norfolk, and bombs from her were heard to drop in the sea. The other followed the Norfolk coast from Trimingham to Great Yarmouth, but did not come overland. Bombs from her were also heard to drop in the sea. Of the four ships which harrowed the north, L.21 traced out a path which enclosed the minor paths traced out by the others. She came in by the Inner Dowsing at a quarter to ten, passed just north of Lincoln, then Sheffield. Turning away from Manchester she was at Bacup at midnight; turning again she began to drop bombs, and went on to Bury and soon after turned about and crossed Bolton, where she dropped nine high explosive and eleven incendiary bombs, which killed thirteen persons, wounded ten, and wrecked a few houses. Leaving Bolton, she skirted Blackburn and then made for Ripon and Whitby. Her last bomb, which was a " dud," was dropped on Bolton Abbey. She passed out to sea at Whitby at three o'clock in the morning. Of the others, L.22 bombed Sheffield, L.14 York, and L.16 nothing in particular. York escaped very lightly. There were no casualties and the damage was negligible. Sheffield fared worse, twenty-nine persons were killed and twenty-one injured. Nine houses were demolished and sixty-two others damaged. On the whole, the manufacturing districts of the north were singled out for attack, but save for the unfortunate casualties the raid effected little or nothing.

Of the fifteen machines up that night, only one, a naval machine from Calshot, saw anything of the airships.

The Germans having now recovered from their London shyness, a resumption of the normal naval practice took place a week later. Eleven ships left their sheds on the afternoon of the 1st October. They were L.13, L.14, L.16, L.17, L.21, L.22, L.23, L.24, L.30, L.31 and the L.34 which had only been delivered a few days previously. One, the L.23, turned back half-way over, and three, the L.13, L.22, and L.30, got near, but did not cross the coast. Of the remaining ships, L.14, L.16 and L.21 raided Lincolnshire, doing no damage whatever. L.24 came over the Norfolk coast and evidently intended to attack London from the north-west on the lines of the attack of 2nd/3rd September. She did not, however, venture beyond Hitchin, where flares of the night landing ground at Willians drew all her bombs, and as a result one man was killed. Her commander then left the country by the most convenient route. The L.34 on her maiden trip did very little—merely making an indefinite journey into the east Midlands. The L.17 penetrated Norfolk and dropped her bombs around Norwich, but without any result.

As for Mathy in the L.31, it was to be his last night, but he went down game to the end. Bringing his ship in at Lowestoft at about eight o'clock, he soon reached Chelmsford. When near Kelvedon Hatch at a quarter to ten, his ship was picked up by searchlights, so he went off north-east past Harlow and was at Buntingford at half-past ten. He now decided to make for his objective from the north, so he swept round to Ware and then turned due south to the descent. At twenty minutes before midnight his ship came under very heavy fire from the guns at Newmans and Temple House. This apparently compelled him to abandon the idea of reaching London, so he dropped most of his bombs, thirty high explosive and twenty-six incendiary, at Cheshunt. These damaged over three hundred dwelling-houses as well as breaking a great many glasshouses. There was only one casualty, however—one woman injured. The airship then went off westward, twisting and turning, rising and falling to avoid the lights, the guns and aeroplanes, which had risen to attack her.

Of several airmen up that night, Second Lieutenant W. J. Tempest had left the ground at North Weald Bassett at ten o'clock for the patrol at Hainault farm—Joyce Green. He was at a height of about 14,500 feet at a quarter to twelve, when he noticed the searchlights to the north of London " concentrated in an enormous pyramid." Following them up to the apex he saw a small " cigar shaped object," which he at once recognised as a Zeppelin and which he estimated to be some fifteen miles off. He then flew full speed at his objective, passing through an " inferno of bursting shells " from the guns below. He drew up close, then dived straight at the airship, firing a burst into her as he approached ; then another as he passed under. He next manœuvred into position under her tail, and flying along underneath her " pumped lead into her " for all he was worth. In his own words:

" As I was firing, I noticed her begin to go red inside like an enormous Chinese lantern, and then a flame shot out of the front part of her and I realised she was on fire."

Tempest had to dive full out to get out of the way of the flaming mass which appeared to be " tearing " after him and which shot past him " roaring like a furnace." After firing a few Very lights, Tempest began to feel " sick and giddy and exhausted," and had considerable difficulty in finding his way to the ground through the fog. On landing he crashed and wrecked his machine, but he himself escaped with a cut on the head. The L.31 fell at Potters Bar just before midnight and with her perished the redoubtable Mathy and his crew. This was the saddest and most serious loss which the German naval airship service ever suffered. The fall of Mathy must have been seen by many of his comrades

L

—certainly by the commander of the L.24—and no doubt their subsequent movements were considerably affected by their leader's tragic fate. With the burning of the L.31 Mathy's last raid petered out.

Airship hunting, which had hitherto been an adventure, was fast becoming a sport. Soon it would provide target practice for tyros.

CHAPTER XIII

THE DECLINE OF THE ZEPPELIN

THE fall of the " thirties " following hot foot on that of the Schutte Lanz was a blow from which the German airship service never recovered. Its Zeppelins were now Frankenstein monsters fast devouring the personnel and material which had gone to their creation. The military service was the first to go under. Officers and crews were drafted to the more prosaic but much more useful work of watching from captive balloons, while the material would be used to better purpose for aeroplanes, which were sadly wanting for the defence of the Fatherland.

As far as the naval airship service was concerned, London, the target for which they had so vehemently fought both on paper and in practice, had perforce to be given up entirely. In fact, no airship would ever again turn to London of its own volition and such airships as remained would carry out tentative attacks in districts as remote from London as possible, but this would not save them from the fate of their forerunners.

When even the raiding of England had to be given
up entirely, the troubles of the Zeppelins were not
at an end. Restricting themselves to overseas reconnaissance they still fished in troubled waters. The
British navy would not tolerate them spying on
its movements, so the Zeppelins were relentlessly
attacked both at sea and in their sheds until the
German airship service had become reduced to
complete impotence. The history of war is full
of triumphs and failures, some glorious and some
otherwise, but no failure of modern time compares
with the bursting of Count von Zeppelin's titanic
airship bubble.

Meanwhile in Great Britain the series of successes
achieved by the aeroplanes against the airships led
to more intensive concentration on the aerial arm.
Not only were the defences of the capital strengthened
and reinforced, but machines were made available to
meet attacks wherever they should take place. There
were now eleven home defence squadrons manned
by the Royal Flying Corps. For the local protection of London there was No. 39 Squadron. To
watch the mouth of the Thames there were No. 37
Squadron to the north of the estuary and Nos. 50 and
78 Squadrons to the south. Athwart the inland path
of the raiders approaching London from the Wash
was No. 75 Squadron and near the Norfolk coast was
No. 51 Squadron. The Wash itself was guarded by
No. 38 Squadron, the Humber by No. 33, the Tees
by No. 76, the Tyne by No. 36, while farther north

for Scotland there was No. 77. For use of the
defending aeroplanes a chain of aerodromes and
landing grounds had been constructed throughout
the length of Great Britain, so that patrolling pilots
were nearly always within sight of harbours of refuge.
Close co-operation between guns, searchlights and
aeroplanes had been carefully practised. On the top
of this there was the highly efficient naval air service
with machines stationed round the whole of the
coast from farthest south to farthest north. These
tenaciously sought and fought the raiders at sea, on
entry, and overland. The team work between the
naval and military aerial defenders was brought to
perfection and results were soon to follow.

Eight weeks had elapsed since Mathy fell. Three
new super-Zeppelins as well as the military best
Schutte Lanz had been destroyed over England
since the beginning of September. But although
the German high command knew now the futility
of further raiding, they dare not yet admit to the
German nation that their beloved weapon had not
only failed of its purpose but was struggling for its
very existence. At the end of November an attack
was accordingly organised against the north of
England where it was thought that the opposition
would be less formidable. So in the early afternoon
of the 27th November ten naval airships left their
sheds for England. They were L.13, L.14, L.16,
L.21, L.22, L.24, L.30, L.34, L.35 and L.36, the
last two being on their maiden raid. One turned

back half-way over and two failed to cross our coast-line. The three newest Zeppelins, the L.34, L.35 and L.36, in addition to the L.24, attempted an attack on the Tyne, while a group of five, the L.13, L.14, L.16, L.21 and L.22, concentrated on the industrial Midlands.

To take the Tyneside first. L.34 came inland over Black Hall Rocks at about half-past eleven. She was at once picked up by the Hutton Henry searchlight. She then turned and tried to extinguish the light with bombs. She failed. Second Lieutenant I. V. Pyott, of No. 36 Squadron, who had ascended from Seaton Carew, sighted her coming south and towards him in the beam of the searchlight. He was at about 9,800 feet up, and the Zeppelin appeared to be below. He flew towards the airship, approached amidships and fired as he passed underneath her, but without result. He then followed her for some five miles firing at her all the time. After seventy-one rounds he noticed a small patch in the body of the airship "become incandescent." He thought at first that this indicated machine-gun fire from the airship directed at him, but the patch rapidly spread and the whole ship was soon engulfed in flames. She fell just before midnight in the sea off West Hartlepool. Pyott dived to avoid the burning wreckage, but his face was scorched by the heat of the flaming mass which he estimated to be some 300 yards away from him. Half an hour later all that was left of the L.34

was a scum of oil on the surface of the water. The flare of the burning ship was seen as far north as Matfen, near Morpeth, and as far south as Poppleton, north of York. From the air it was seen by Captain G. H. Birley of No. 38 Squadron at Buckminster, nearly 140 miles off. Just before she caught fire, she began dropping bombs on West Hartlepool. The sixteen which fell, killed four and wounded thirty-four persons and wrecked or damaged some forty houses.

Flight Lieutenant de Roeper, who went up from Redcar also in pursuit of L.34, arrived on the scene after her destruction. The effect of the conflagration of the L.34 on her consorts was terrific. L.35, which had crossed the coast in her company a few miles to the north, turned about and flew quickly away, purposely dropping no bombs to avoid being heard, if perchance she had not already been seen. The L.36 at the time of the disaster had not yet come overland and was groping for the Tyne. Now thoroughly roused she relieved herself of her bombs, and went off. As for the L.24, she was well out at sea and at once turned about.

Of the five Midland raiders, the L.21 embarked that night upon a remarkable career. She came in at Atwick soon after nine o'clock, where she was greeted by the Barmston guns, so she went out to sea again to try her luck farther north. She came in once more and was at Driffield at a quarter to ten, and then described a sinuous curve to Wakefield, near which town her first bombs were dropped. She then passed on to Barnsley, arriving there about midnight and dropped some more bombs nearby. Both these places had been bombed previously by the L.16. An hour later she was at Macclesfield. Next she visited the district west of Hanley, being attracted by the slag heaps at Chesterton, where most of her load was flung overboard. Having now gone far west enough she turned, went via Stoke-upon-Trent, Uttoxeter, Melbourne, Long Eaton, Melton Mowbray, and by a winding path to Great Yarmouth, emerging at six in the morning. She had been overland for nearly nine hours and had long overstayed her welcome. After shaking off two aeroplanes, which had attacked her on her outward course, and throttling down her engines as much as possible to escape detection, her commander may have been relieved when he saw the open sea. Drifting slowly over Lowestoft the L.21 was attacked by many guns from which, however, she escaped injury. She now put on full speed for home. While she had been hurrying across Norfolk, however, the Commodore in charge at Lowestoft and Yarmouth got timely news of her and made his arrangements for the official welcome when she should arrive in his command. Aeroplanes were ordered up from Holt and Bacton respectively at five in the morning.

An hour later Yarmouth reported "Zeppelin overhead," so machines were immediately despatched

from Burgh Castle and Yarmouth. In the dawn
which was breaking, the aeroplanes could see and
clearly follow the airship. Flight Lieutenant E.
Cadbury and Flight Sub-Lieutenant G. W. R. Fane
from Burgh Castle were soon on L.21's track, while
Flight Sub-Lieutenant E. L. Pulling from Bacton
also joined in the pursuit.

Soon after half-past six, when the Zeppelin was
about 8,000 feet up and some nine miles off Lowestoft, she was overtaken. Cadbury got under her at
about 700 feet range and fired into her afterpart.
He exhausted his ammunition into her body, but
without apparent effect. Fane then took up the
cudgels and attempted to fire her at about 100 feet
range, but his gun jammed at the critical moment.
Now was the time for the third musketeer. Pulling
advanced to within sixty feet and opened fire at
once. After ten rounds the Zeppelin caught fire and
within a few seconds was "nothing but a fiery furnace." All three aviators had been under heavy
machine-gun fire from the airship, which even continued to fire at Pulling for an appreciable time after
he had set her ablaze. The L.21 fell stern foremost
into the sea where she was engulfed, leaving nothing
but oil to mark her watery grave. The fate of the
L.21 had thus been foredoomed. She had failed to
profit from the lessons of her two predecessors—
the L.19 and the L.20. Like them, she had courted
disaster by attempting the impossible. To linger
for more than a few hours over England was beyond

the capacity of the airships of the time, and to be caught in the light of day was flirting with death. Of the others, L.14 ventured Hull, but was deterred by guns and aeroplanes. L.13 made York, which she bombed to little purpose. L.16 harried Wakefield and Barnsley, and L.22 did nothing in particular. As might be expected, the destruction of the two airships in this raid had the now familiar sequel. For an expenditure of over two hundred bombs there were only four fatal casualties and thirty-seven persons injured. The damage was trivial.

It was now fully brought home to the Germans that in a combat between an aeroplane and an airship the dice were loaded against the lighter-than-air vessel, and unless the airship could get completely out of reach of the aeroplane she ceased to be of any military use whatsoever. Thus began the frantic struggle for more height. In the next ships to be laid down—the L.43 class—the ceiling was increased to about 18,000 feet by a ruthless cutting down of weight, and by the employment of engines specially designed to maintain their power in the rarefied atmosphere in which they were to work. But all to no avail as the aeroplane was developing at a faster rate. Moreover, exposure at such heights had serious effects on the crews. The cold was intense, air sickness supervened and oxygen had to be breathed artificially. But their troubles did not cease with these. At very great heights

treacherous wind changes and most unexpected
gales are apt to be encountered, although at lower
altitudes perfect calm may prevail, just as when the
surface of the sea is most troubled, perfect peace
reigns at the bottom. These forces also played
their part in the eventual débâcle. The remnants
of Germany's most vaunted air-borne fleet were
soon to be submerged. Nothing could save
them.

The Zeppelins had done their best and their worst.
They had been launched for the offensive in the
fateful days of 1915, and their attacks had increased
in intensity and vigour until they had reached their
heyday in the fall of 1916. But our defences forced
them into a precarious position. Having been struck
down by our aeroplanes the airship raiders were
soon to give way to their own. Such further attacks
as would fall to their lot would only be delivered in
the paroxysms of approaching extinction. But they
had managed to do us grievous harm, albeit insignificant in proportion to the hopes excited and the
efforts expended. To begin with, the Zeppelin
menace had compelled us to retain at home some
twelve flying squadrons and thereby weakened our
air force in the main and other theatres of war.
Also, the very considerable number of anti-aircraft
guns and searchlights needed for their discomfiture
seriously affected the supply of these weapons to
theatres of war sadly in need of them. As many
as 400 guns were earmarked for home defence to

meet the onslaughts of the airships. More serious
still was the retention at home of personnel skilled
in anti-aircraft defence. These at the end of 1916
totalled some 17,000, of which some 200 officers
and 2,000 men manned the dozen flying squadrons.
In addition there were the not inconsiderable naval
machines and personnel who watched and guarded
the coast. But all this cannot be put entirely to
the account of the Zeppelins. The year 1916 was
one in which the military strength of the enemy was
a considerable factor. If Germany ever contemplated
an invasion of Great Britain either as a demonstration
or worse, 1916 was the time when such a project
had any chance at all. Then it was thought that
the Germans might be able to find a force of some
160,000 men of all arms for an invasion of the British
Isles. Although the difficulties for the enemy of
such an attempt were well nigh insuperable, there
was the fact to be faced that if the Germans believed
that such an operation would offer reasonable prospects of ending the war they would undoubtedly
undertake it. Whatever may be the theoretical
aspect, such a project had not only to be considered
as possible, but measures had to be devised for the
contingency.

During the period in question, a total force of
nearly half a million was specifically organised in
this country to provide garrison troops and anti-
aircraft defences. Clearly an air force was a vital
necessity in any scheme for repelling invasion.

Not only was it required for patrol and observation, but as an offensive weapon, first, against a hostile disembarkation, and secondly, against any air forces which the enemy might try to establish or maintain on our soil. So that in considering the retention of so vast a number of squadrons at home, the lesser real danger of the airships to which we were exposed must not be allowed to obscure the greater menace of invasion for which provision had to be made.

During 1915 there were twenty airship attacks in which a total weight of thirty-seven tons of bombs was dropped on our soil or round our shores. These killed 207 persons and wounded 533. In 1916 the airship raids numbered twenty-two and the bombs dropped weighed in all 125 tons. This vast mass of missiles killed 293 persons and wounded 691. For the rest of the war the eleven attacks were productive of fifty-six deaths and injuries to 134 persons, the bombs thrown totalling some forty-four tons. Although material damage was small and relatively unimportant, the indirect effects were serious. On receipt of raid warnings, and there were many false alarms, work was suspended, sometimes over vast industrial areas, traffic was disorganised, and an adverse moral effect was produced both on the workers and on the population. As a broad result some one-sixth of the total normal output of munitions was entirely lost and the quality of a less proportion was affected. It is not surprising, therefore, that the Germans were loath to abandon the air raids on Great

Britain. If the airship had become useless and even obsolete for the purpose, the alternative was near at hand and almost ready. The cumbersome Zeppelins were eclipsed by the smaller and more compact aeroplanes. These, even if they could not transport such great loads of bombs or carry these missiles so far, at any rate operating from bases in Belgium, they could reach and harry London, and, moreover, could be employed in large numbers. Further, they were not necessarily compelled to shun the light of day for which, however, they showed scant appreciation.

While these heavier-than-air attacks were being planned and perfected, the airships carried on as best they could. Meanwhile the London gun defences were being re-organised. At the end of 1916 there were seven ground formations in and immediately round the capital. Six were manned by the Royal Artillery and Royal Engineer personnel. They were situated at Dartford, Woolwich, Hilly Fields, Putney, Wembley, and Waltham. For central London there was the Naval Volunteer Corps with headquarters in Whitehall. Seven separate commands were found to be somewhat too decentralised so they were reduced to four—north at Waltham, east at Woolwich, west at Putney, and central. Further, they were placed under the command of Colonel Simon, the newly-created Anti-Aircraft Defence Commander of London. Various improvements were also introduced. A uniform system of obtaining and passing intelligence with a compact code for rapidity was brought out, and guns and searchlights were provided with devices for accurately plotting the courses of hostile aircraft. Searchlights were instructed to work on a specified system co-operating with one another. The general scheme was that guns and searchlights were to be used without hesitation and to open at long range. Their primary object was to drive off the enemy, his destruction being secondary. By the throwing up of London searchlights *en masse* and maintaining a rigorous patrol of the London skies the boldest airship commanders would be deterred. They knew from experience that umbrage afforded the only hope of refuge; the searchlights' rays were to them the rays of death.

The resumption of the airship attacks in 1917 was feeble in the extreme. On the night of the 16th February, the L.Z.107, a military airship, after having raided Calais crossed the Straits of Dover and made the English coast. She was over Deal at about two in the morning and was last heard going out to sea a quarter of an hour later via Ramsgate. No bombs were dropped and she gave the defences neither time nor opportunity for attacking her. The object of this abortive effort is unknown. A month later the naval service came again into action. The raiding squadron comprised five of the most recent ships, the L.35, L.39, L.40, L.41, and L.42, and these set out on the 16th March. L.42 did not attempt to raid. She hugged the Dutch coast and then crossed Belgium, making for home after cruising about for nearly two hours in the vicinity of Zeebrugge. The others came in and bombed Kent and a bit of Sussex to no purpose. There were no casualities whatever, and damage done was infinitesimal in spite of the seventy-nine bombs that were counted. Strong winds completely upset the plan of attack. Thick clouds interfered with the raiders as they also did with our searchlights. The airships could not see where they were, and the searchlights, being unable to penetrate the cloud bank, could not help our aeroplanes to find the enemy. Second Lieutenant D. D. Fowler of No. 78 Squadron at Telescombe Cliffs in Sussex, crashed in his B.E.2E one and half miles from the aerodrome and was killed.

On the way home the raiding ariships lost their sense of direction and badly floundered. With no hope of reaching their bases by the North Sea route they tried to win home overland across France or Belgium. The L.35, L.40 and L.41 which set the best courses, eventually got there, though with great difficulty. Two reached their sheds, but the L.35 was driven by the wind far into central Germany and finally reached Dresden in a crippled condition. Had it not been for a cloudy sky they would undoubtedly have suffered a similar fate to that which befell the L.39. This ship came in at Margate at about half-past ten and went out at St. Leonards

about an hour later. Crossing the Channel in a
south-easterly direction, her commander, Kapitanleutnant Koch, brought her over the French coast by
Dieppe. Continuing on his course, he reached the
Seine, north of Mantes, at about four in the morning.
Turning north, Koch reached Gisors, then struck
Beauvais, where he was picked up by searchlights
and fired at by an anti-aircraft battery. He accele-
rated and reached Froissy at about five in the morning. As dawn was now approaching, Koch seems to
have decided that the only safe way of getting over
the French lines was to cut out his engines and
drift with the wind. At about half-past five his
ship was observed hovering over Compiegne. Here
the L.39 was assailed by violent anti-aircraft fire
and was shot down in flames from a height of some
10,000 feet, and with her perished Koch and his
crew.

Next there was a hiatus for over two months,
ending on the 23rd May, when six naval ships once
again essayed England. It would appear that London was about to be braved by the Great Eastern
railway route from Harwich to London. But the
commanders had their eyes to the Wash. Only one
ship, the L.42, made any serious effort to approach
the capital. Dietrich I came in at Walton-on-the-
Naze after midnight. After a vague westerly advance
he arrived at Braintree. Leaving the troubled atmosphere on his port beam he set a course calculated
to increase his distance from London in the shortest

M

possible time. He went north. When nearing the coast of Norfolk, towards Cromer, he very nearly ran into the trouble which he had been at such pains to avoid earlier. No. 51 Squadron's aeroplanes were looking for him but missed him in the low clouds. He got away. Little need be said of the others. One did not come over at all; one merely got a foothold near Great Yarmouth; one traversed a little of Norfolk; and the other two made a voyage in the safe preserves of Suffolk and Norfolk. The timorous tactics of the raid is reflected in the result. One man was killed, and trifling damage was done to farm-houses and cottages by the two tons of bombs dropped on land. Many machines rose to the attack, but mist and cloud favoured the raiders and obscured them from view.

A naval seaplane from Westgate which went up to engage the raiders in the early hours of the 24th became overdue but was later found and towed into Grain. Meanwhile another seaplane, piloted by Flight Sub-Lieutenant H. M. Morris, with Air Mechanic G. O. Wright as wireless operator, left the station in search of the missing machine. After spending some hours over the North Sea, Morris started for home. A failing engine, however, compelled him to land some thirty miles out to sea in one of our minefields. There were no ships in sight and very little chance of any approaching that area. After a time Morris got rid of his bombs and his petrol to lighten the labouring seaplane. But a rough sea wrought havoc with his machine, and in the early afternoon the tail sank into the water and the machine turned on its back to be torn to pieces by the raging sea. Morris and his hapless companion managed to get on to an undamaged float, hanging on to such fittings as would give them a hold. The float was watertight, but was tossed mercilessly by the waves and the shipwrecked aviators were constrained to lie across it, half in and half out of the water. Incredible although it may appear, Morris and Wright spent five nights on their precarious perch. Eventually they were rescued on the 29th May by a Large America seaplane on patrol in the North Sea, but not without further adventure as the rescuers' machine failed to rise and had in turn to be rescued by surface craft. Within two months Morris and Wright were again flying.

An interesting feature of this raid was the despatch of a Large America seaplane from Yarmouth to Terschelling to intercept and destroy the returning airships. The boat left Yarmouth shortly after four in the morning with Flight Lieutenant C. J. Galpin and Flight Sub-Lieutenant R. Leckie as pilots. After patrolling around Borkum Riff and seeing no airships they made for home at about half-past six. Soon after they turned, a Zeppelin appeared out of the clouds at some 2,000 feet, about a mile away and coming towards them. They immediately made to attack, but owing to clouds were unable to get close up and such fire as they could bring to bear was ineffective. Shortage of petrol compelled them reluctantly to give up the chase.

The next attack took place on the 17th June, when four naval ships made the attempt. Two, however, turned back without crossing the coast. One, the L.42, bombed Ramsgate about two in the morning, causing considerable damage. A naval ammunition store was blown up and buildings were destroyed by fire. Three persons were killed and sixteen injured. The airship eluded the defences and got away. The other ship which raided was the L.48. She was under the command of Kapitanleutnant Eichler and had on board Korvettenkapitan Schutze, the Commodore of the North Sea Airship Division. She came in at Orfordness at about two in the morning, rounded Wickham Market, and then went south past Woodbridge. She dropped bombs in the vicinity of Martlesham with little effect. She was then heavily engaged by anti-aircraft guns both on shore and on ships close by. She evidently intended to attack Harwich, but appears to have been diverted from her objective to the north. Second Lieutenant L. P. Watkins of No. 37 Squadron, who went up from Goldhanger just after two o'clock in the morning, was at a height of about 11,000 feet over Harwich when he " saw the A.A. guns firing and several searchlights pointing towards the same spot." Almost at once he sighted the L.48 about 2,000 feet above him. He immediately

ZEPPELIN L.11.—Commissioned 7th June, 1915. Carried out 29 reconnaissances and 12 raids. Became a training ship and was broken up on 5th April, 1917

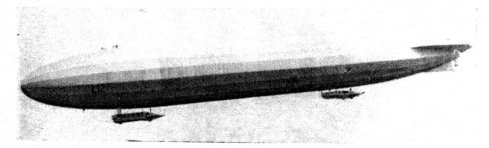

ZEPPELIN L.12.—Commissioned 21st June, 1915. Carried out 5 reconnaissances. Came down on 10th August, 1915, after being hit on her first raid

ZEPPELIN L.30.—Commissioned 30th May, 1916. Carried out 27 reconnaissances and 10 raids. Placed out of commission 17th November, 1917. Ultimately broken up in October, 1920, and delivered to Belgium

[*Photographs from Dr. Eckener's lecture on " Modern Zeppelin Airships." Reproduced by courtesy of the Royal Aeronautical Society*]

ZEPPELIN L.48.—Commissioned 23rd May, 1917. Carried out one reconnaissance. Was brought down in England on 17th June, 1917, on first raid.

The blackening of the underside was to render the ship less visible at night.

To face p. 166

climbed up towards her, firing two drums in succession into her tail without effect. Having now reached 13,200 feet he was still some 500 feet below the L.48. Three short bursts were followed by the remainder of the drum and " the Zeppelin burst into flames at the tail." The L.48 fell flaming into a field at Holly Tree farm near Theberton. Captain R. H. M. S. Saundby, of the Experimental Station at Orfordness, had engaged the airship about the same time. He believed that it was his ammunition that fired her, but the *coup de grâce* appears to have been given by Watkins.

L.48 did not come down with the rapidity usual in such catastrophes, the fall taking from three to five minutes, and to this comparatively slow fall three survivors owed their lives. The airship came down stern first at an angle of about sixty degrees, smashing the whole afterpart, including the rear gondola, all the occupants of which were killed. The front gondola was badly damaged, but of its occupants, one, Leutnant Mieth, survived, though terribly injured. The two men in the side gondolas also survived, one severely injured and the other unhurt. According to the survivors, the airmen's attack was unexpected as they believed that they were a few miles off Harwich on their way home. When the ship began to fall, her officers fully expected that she would come down on water, and Eichler, her commander, quietly took off his leather surcoat and began to remove his overalls with the obvious intention of swimming for life, Schutze, the flag officer in the forward gondola, clutched the edge of the map table, while hideous screams issued from the burning part of the ship.

CHAPTER XIV

OVERSEA ZEPPELIN HUNTING AND THE SILENT RAID

SAVE for an abortive effort on the 21st August no further airships came to the attack until the end of September, the raiding season of the summer of 1917 being given over to the aeroplanes. But meantime, while the Zeppelins confined themselves to overseas patrol, the British navy set itself the task of putting out the eyes of the German High Seas Fleet. When suitable flying boats, capable of extended overseas flight became available, they were at first employed for reconnaissance and submarine hunting. But in the spring of 1917 a number of Large America seaplanes at Felixstowe, at Yarmouth and at Killingholme were specially detailed to hunt down and destroy reconnoitring Zeppelins. Timely knowledge of the whereabouts of these airships was essential for the success of the chase, and special arrangements were made for rapidly passing information as to airship activity to the naval air

stations. On receiving warning, machines were at
once despatched to the attack up to a distance of
150 miles. So accordingly on the 14th May, 1917,
although thick mist obscured the sea under a lowering
sky, a Large America seaplane, manned by Flight
Lieutenant C. J. Galpin, Flight Sub-Lieutenant
R. Leckie, Chief Petty Officer V. F. Whatling and
Air Mechanic O. R. Laycock, set out from Yarmouth
to destroy a Zeppelin which had been located near
the Terschelling lightvessel. When about eighty
miles had been covered, the boat broke off wireless
communication with her base in order to prevent
discovery by the enemy. After a further half an
hour's flight, the Zeppelin was sighted coming
towards them, but some ten miles away. Slowly
patrolling, she appeared blissfully unconscious of
the flying boat which was rapidly approaching,
unseen by the airship, against a background of a
cloud of fog. The Zeppelin, apparently having
reached the end of her beat, turned about, but the
boat overhauled her at about five o'clock and came
up to within fifty yards. Galpin then opened a
devastating fire from the forward cockpit, but his
two guns jammed in succession, so the boat was
turned away to enable him to rectify the stoppages.
But the deadly work had already been done. While
the boat was turning, a glowing light was noticed
right in the middle of the airship, and within a minute
she was in flames. Plunging into the sea she left
on the surface a mass of black ash from which

sprang up and stood a column of brown smoke about 1,500 feet high. This marked the end of the L.22.

Next, on the 14th June, 1917, a Large America from Felixstowe, engaged on a similar mission, was off Vlieland at about nine in the morning, when the L.43 was sighted about five miles away and temptingly low at about 1,500 feet. Flight Sub-Lieutenant B. D. Hobbs was piloting. He put on full speed, quickly rose from 500 to 2,000 feet, and dived on to the tail of the unsuspecting airship. The midship gun, manned by the wireless operator, H. M. Davis, opened the fire, and while passing diagonally across the airship's tail, Flight Sub-Lieutenant R. F. L. Dickey, the second pilot, fired from the bow guns. Two bursts were sufficient. The airship flared up. Three men were seen to fall out on her way down, and the wreckage was observed to burn for some time on the water. Success had only been possible with surprise, and after these two disasters the airships were no longer to be found at low altitudes, and the airship commanders became more watchful; so no further successes of this kind followed in the immediate future. In fact, only one more Zeppelin suffered at the hands of the flying boats, and this nearly a year later.

Meanwhile also the experience of Flight Lieutenant Freeman, who it will be recalled flew a Bristol Scout off the *Vindex* on the 2nd August,

1916, in an attempt to bring down a Zeppelin, was fully exploited. One result was the fitting out of light cruisers with platforms in the forward part of the weather deck to enable aeroplanes to rise from them at sea. The first vessel to be so fitted was H.M.S. *Yarmouth*, and it was found that a Sopwith " Pup " could successfully take the air from the platform. The practical value of this was soon to be demonstrated. On the 21st August, 1917, at half-past four in the morning, H.M.S. *Yarmouth*, in company with the First Light Cruiser Squadron, was engaged on a sweeping operation off the Danish coast. Near Lyngvig a Zeppelin was sighted south-westward in company with a seaplane. As the airship was not far from her base, the squadron continued on a northerly course to entice her away. The *Yarmouth* was kept carefully closed up at the rear of the formation not to excite any suspicion; the sting was in the tail. The Zeppelin rose to the bait and followed. An hour later, when the Lodbjerg light was abeam and the airship was still keeping the squadron company some twelve miles to the westward, a turn was made into the wind, and after steaming thus about two miles, the order was sent to the *Yarmouth* to " fly her aeroplane." A few minutes later Flight Sub-Lieutenant B. A. Smart got his Sopwith " Pup " in the air. He climbed to 7,000 feet and flew straight for the airship some fifteen miles away. He got above, apparently unobserved, and diving on to her tail gave her a

burst of some fifteen rounds from his Lewis gun
As his bullets missed the mark he next got within
twenty yards and fired another burst into the airship's
stern. This time the shots got home, for flames
shot out of the airship and immediately her after
end became a roaring furnace which Smart had
difficulty in avoiding. The flames quickly spread;
the airship crumpled up, plunged into the sea and
burnt herself out. All that was left to mark the
fate of the L.23 was a few charred specks on the
surface of the sea. Smart had never before risen
from the *Yarmouth's* platform, and he was the
first to bring down an airship by an aeroplane
flown from a light cruiser. His task accomplished,
Smart set course for his mother ship some
ten miles away. He landed in the sea and was
promptly picked up by a boat from H.M.S. *Prince*.
In all, only fifty-nine minutes had elapsed since
he rose from the *Yarmouth*. The Commodore, in
his report, says that " Smart could not have accomplished the destruction in quicker or more business-
like manner." It was truly one crowded glorious
hour.

It might have been supposed that the Zeppelins
had had enough for that day, but with admirable
persistence, the German naval airship service came
over in force to raid England that evening, probably
to avenge the loss of the L.23. Eight Zeppelins
left Germany for the attack, the squadron being
commanded by Strasser himself. The fleet made

for the Yorkshire coast, bound, apparently, for Hull. Arrived within fifty or sixty miles of the Humber, the airships hung about for three hours; then about midnight one essayed an attack on Hull. This was the only vessel which actually crossed the coast. She came in at Tunstall about midnight and wandered about for an hour and a half between the coast and the Humber. Her commander was evidently unprepared to face the guns, searchlights or aeroplanes, so his bombs were dropped more or less promiscuously. They proved sacrilegious, as they demolished two chapels, one Primitive Methodist and the other Roman Catholic, and in addition damaged a Y.M.C.A. hut. There was no loss of life and only one man was injured. She was chased out to sea for twenty miles by Lieutenant H. P. Solomon of No. 33 Squadron, who had risen from Scampton. When in the neighbourhood of Beverley, at a height of 15,000 feet, he saw the airship and set off in pursuit, but could not keep pace with her and follow her upwards at the same time. In all, nineteen aeroplanes swarmed to attack the airship, but she got away, thanks to her height. Her luck was great, as a Large America from Killingholme also went to intercept her in her own waters, but failed to sight her.

After an interval of over a month a further attempt was made. Ten ships crossed the North Sea separately during the late afternoon of the 24th September, 1917, and concentrated east of Flamborough Head, just as they had done in the preceding raid. After hovering or cruising about this area until darkness, the formation broke up, each ship to its separate task except one which went home. Five ships actually attacked; four of them came well overland and one pushed in as far as the Rotherham district of south Yorkshire. There were many factors which militated against the success of both the airships and the defenders. The sky was cloudy, and this, coupled with the extreme height of the raiding airships, rendered accurate location of objectives out of the question. At the same time it afforded them protection from the aeroplanes. With the exception of Hull, which was carefully sought for and found, the commanders seem to have had no objectives in view and shed their bombs on any bright lights they could see. Thus the airship that went to Rotherham made a direct rush in the direction of an ironworks and colliery, but the lights there were doused in time and the bombs meant for their destruction fell innocuously in fields. Two other ships attacked the landing flares at three aerodromes in Lincolnshire, wasting their bombs to no purpose. Another ship sought the familiar Skinningrove works, but was driven off by guns before she could do any damage. Even Hull itself escaped lightly. Although eleven bombs were dropped fair in the centre of the city only three women were slightly injured and the damage done was insignificant.

Of the thirty-seven aeroplanes that rose to attack the raiders that night, few sighted any of the airships. Lieutenant W. W. Cook, of No. 76 Squadron, left Helperby at about one in the morning to patrol between that aerodrome and Shipton. He encountered a strong south-westerly wind, thick mist and low clouds, and when at a height of 2,000 feet he could not see the aerodrome flares or any other ground lights. On perceiving searchlights to the north-east he made in that direction and found himself over Middlesbrough. He was then 10,000 feet up and saw a Zeppelin some 6,000 feet above him held by searchlights and fired at by guns. Soon, however, the airship managed to evade the lights and so Cook had to give up the chase. A strong westerly wind of some sixty miles an hour was fast blowing him out to sea, so, steering a south-westerly course, he made to return to his patrol line. After some fifty minutes he found himself over Atwick at some 14,500 feet. Here he observed another Zeppelin held in searchlight beams to the north of Hull. This ship was also some 16,000 feet up, and before Cook could get within striking range the lights were switched off and so once again he lost his target. Carrying on with a coastal patrol he sighted a third Zeppelin by the light of approaching dawn. He immediately gave chase and this time managed to get within 800 yards of his prey into which he fired four drums of ammunition, but apparently without effect. Although he hung on the airship until he was sixty miles out to sea he was unable to catch her up again. Even so he continued to look for others until at five in the morning he decided it was time to make for home. Struggling against the strong westerly wind it was an hour and a quarter before he sighted land. He had just enough petrol to make the coast at Flamborough Head and landed safely in a field a quarter of a mile from the shore. His adventures in the air extended over five hours.

Second Lieutenant C. Pinnock, of No. 33 Squadron, who went up from Elsham in an F.E.2D., struck a tree when landing and his observer, Lieutenant J. A. Menzies, was killed. From No. 36 Squadron an F.E.2D., which rose from Seaton Carew, failed to return. The pilot was Second Lieutenant H. J. Thornton and the observer Second Lieutenant C. A. Moore.

The Zeppelins had overreached themselves. Forced to seek greater and still greater heights they found themselves helpless in the fury of the vast and unlimited ocean of air. The frail aircraft were shaken and buffeted in gales which on the sea would shiver the timbers of the stoutest ships. The wonder is that not so many were wrecked, but that so many survived. If an engine stopped, even momentarily, it was immediately frozen up and so much less power was available for the struggle against relentless and unbridled forces. Should the crews attempt to attend to their multifarious duties they found themselves unable to do so. Height sickness and intense cold paralysed them and rendered them impotent. Under such conditions the Zeppelins—in normal circumstances so graceful and responsive—became so much flotsam and jetsam in an ocean of fury. These were the conditions which eleven naval airships set out to face, knowingly or not, on the 19th October, 1917. The destination of the squadron appears to have been the industrial centre of England. No attack on so vast a scale had been attempted in that region since the great attack against the Midlands of January, 1916, and in point of number of airships employed it was only surpassed by the fateful raid of the 2nd September, 1916.

On the night in question the weather conditions were such that while perfect calm reigned over the surface of England and the North Sea, with increase of altitude light north-westerly winds prevailed in the region of 10,000 feet, and above that height the wind suddenly increased to some forty miles an hour and progressively higher up, so that at 20,000 feet, the only safe height for raiding airships, it was blowing a gale from north and north-west. The raiding airships which made their landfalls at various points at the Humber, the Lincolnshire coast, the Wash and the northern coast of Norfolk, were caught in this wind, and, in spite of all endeavours westward towards the north Midlands, they were forced to the south-east. One ship alone, the L.54, returned straight home across the North Sea. Three made their way either along the Dutch coast or across Holland back to Germany; three more crossed Northern France and reached their own country over the Allied lines between Ypres and Luneville. The remaining four airships, L.44, L.45, L.49, and L.50 were driven southward in their endeavour to make their way east, and were either destroyed or surrendered.

Take the various airships in turn. L.41, commanded by Hauptmann Manger, approached the mouth of the Humber at about seven o'clock. She was at once fired on by H.M.S. *Albion*. She passed the Spurn and went inland over Cleethorpes. She then went to Waltham, to Caistor and to Holton-le-Moor, where she dropped a petrol tank. Passing on south-westward she threw two bombs north of Lincoln, which killed two sheep. She was next at Derby, in the neighbourhood of which she circled about slowly for an hour and a half. She then went off and an hour later appeared slightly to west of Birmingham. Here she dropped a series of bombs, but only slight damage was done, chiefly to the unwarned Austin motor works, which were fully lit up. The airship then went over Redditch and was next observed to the south of Northampton where she dropped two " dud " bombs. At midnight she passed Castle Thorpe. Continuing on her south-easterly course she eventually spanned the Thames estuary from Shoeburyness to Whitstable and finally

N

out to sea by Walmer. Crossing the Straits of Dover, she went into France by Gravelines and then for nearly three hours circled about over the zone of the Belgian and British armies. Finally she crossed the lines near La Bassee and across Belgium and into Germany.

The L.44, commanded by Kapitanleutnant Stabbert, entered the Wash at about half-past seven, rounded Boston and then followed the Great Northern railway via Spalding, Peterborough and Bedford. Here she dropped ten bombs in a line between Elstow and Kempston. These narrowly missed a large ammunition dump, but two men were injured. She then went west towards Wolverton, but soon turned to the south-east, in which direction she persisted. Ten bombs were dropped near Leighton Buzzard to no purpose. Next she passed Luton, St. Albans, Hatfield, Brentwood, Purfleet, Gravesend and so to Maidstone, at which place the flares of Detling aerodrome attracted her attention. These she bombed, the aerodrome was missed and the bombs did little harm. The airship then made for Canterbury and finally went out to sea between Folkestone and Dover at half-past eleven under fire from many guns. Twenty minutes later she passed Boulogne, and was then carried inland on a more or less south-easterly course. At a quarter-past one in the morning she was at Montdidier, and a little time after at Reims. Thence she passed Bar le Duc reached the neighbourhood of Luneville and next

came within range of the anti-aircraft guns at
Vathimenil, being then at some 11,000 feet. In
spite of her strenuous attempt to rise she was finally
hit at some 19,000 feet. The airship immediately
took fire and fell to the ground at Chenevieres.
L.44 was reduced to a mass of half calcined girders,
and all on board perished.

L.45, commanded by Kapitanleutnant Kölle,
came over the Yorkshire coast near Withernsea at
about half-past eight. Her course was considerably
interfered with by defending aeroplanes but she was
able to elude them by rising. She crossed the Humber and was at Louth at quarter-past nine, and next
dropped a petrol tank to the south of Lincoln. Half
an hour later she was near Leicester, some 15,000
feet up, and was attacked by an aeroplane a thousand
feet below, but without apparent result. The airship next reached Northampton shortly before
eleven. Here she dropped her main load of bombs,
but little damage resulted. From Northampton she
followed the London and North-Western railway
line right to London. She announced her presence
by dropping bombs at Hendon and Cricklewood.
Next one fell in Piccadilly. This killed seven persons and wounded eighteen. It also made a large
hole in the roadway near Swan and Edgar's. The
airship then went on south-eastward and dropped
two large bombs, one at Camberwell and one at
Hither Green. Twenty-four people were killed and
thirty injured as a result of these two 300 kilogramme

missiles, and many houses were demolished or damaged.

The airship went on eastward, and shortly after midnight, when just south of the Medway, was attacked by Lieutenant T. B. Pritchard of No. 39 Squadron, but he was baffled by her height, although he followed her for over half an hour. The airship passed out to sea at Hastings shortly before one in the morning, and crossing the Channel, she reached the French coast at about Berck-sur-Mer. Carried by the wind she passed Amiens, Compiegne, and at a quarter-past six was over Auxerre. Here she came under fire but was out of range of the guns. Proceeding, she reached Lyon where Kölle seems to have become cognisant of his whereabouts, and he made several attempts to beat north-eastward to gain Switzerland, since he had not sufficient petrol left to regain Germany.

When over the snow-topped Haute Alpes, Kölle apparently thought he was over his goal. Crippled with engine failure the L.45 was harried by several French aeroplanes, but they failed to shoot her down. At about ten in the morning Kölle, believing himself now in Switzerland, had reached Sisteron; he realised that he must either land or perish, so he circled over the town in full view of the interned officers of the L.Z.85, which had been brought down at Salonika eighteen months before. When looking about for a suitable landing-place Kölle soon saw that he was still in France. But too late—he had

Damage caused by a 2-cwt. bomb which was dropped at a venture by the Zeppelin L.45 and which fell outside Messrs. Swan & Edgar's premises in Piccadilly during the "Silent Raid" on the night of the 19th October, 1917. The casualties from this bomb were seven people killed and eighteen others injured   *To face p.* 182

run out of petrol. Finding a good spot he made to land, but when the airship touched the ground she was caught by a gust of wind which heeled her over. A car with its two occupants came away and two other men jumped from another. Lightened of this weight, the L.45 rose and was again caught by the wind. She finally dashed against the eastern side of the valley of the Beuche, whereupon the occupants jumped to the ground. Kölle and his crew fired their ship and then surrendered, greatly exhausted after their prolonged flight.

L.46, commanded by Kapitanleutnant Hollender, merely brushed the north-eastern part of Norfolk. Her bombs fell at Walcot and East Ruston. They killed two horses and did little else. She got home via Holland. The L.47, commanded by Kapitanleutnant von Freudenreich, came in at a quarter to eight by Sutton-on-Sea. She zig-zagged to Castle Bytham and then followed a south-easterly course which brought her out to sea at Walton-on-the-Naze. Bombs were dropped en route, but without effect. She went away via Ostend, Flushing, Zeeland, crossed the Zuyder Zee, gained the Frisian Islands and so reached home.

L.49, commanded by Kapitanleutnant Gayer, came in at Holkham at eight o'clock. She flew south on an irregular course, dropped her main load of bombs between East Dereham and Wymondham to little purpose, and came out at Frinton. She then crossed to Margate, and finally out to sea at Sandgate. She next entered France at Cape Grisnez and was driven past Arras, St. Quentin, Laon, Reims, Bar-le-Duc and Neufchateau to Epinal, where she appeared soon after six in the morning. Here she was attacked by five French aeroplanes and was forced by them to land in the valley of Apance. Gayer attempted to fire his ship, but was prevented, and so a perfectly good Zeppelin of the latest type fell into the hands of the French.

L.50, commanded by Kapitanleutnant Schwonder, came in at Cley-next-the-Sea at a quarter to eight. She reached Stoke Ferry, turned south-east, passed to Stowmarket and out to sea at Hollesley Bay just before nine. Her load of bombs was dropped from west of Swaffham to Thetford but did no harm whatever. She entered France over Dunkirk at eleven and went on to Dixmude and thence over the German sector by Valenciennes and Guise, without knowing it. Next she crossed the French lines in the Champagne. Owing to the thick fog her commander had no idea of his whereabouts. He wandered on tortuously, and eventually came to the region of Epinal. Here he was attacked by French aeroplanes, but escaped. Later Schwonder saw the L.49 resting on the ground beneath him, and believing himself now to be in friendly territory, he made to land. Coming down he realised his mistake and forced his ship up to 10,000 feet, but almost immediately brought her down again. The forward car was torn off by some trees. Sixteen men in all left the ship at this juncture, and the ship released of this weight shot up into the air and disappeared. The derelict hull of the L.50 now became the sport of the wind. On her path to the Mediterranean she was repeatedly attacked by aeroplanes without result. She drifted over Sisteron, where she was seen by the interned officers of the L.Z. 85. She was finally seen drifting out to sea near Frejus at about half-past five in the afternoon and was pursued till nightfall by seaplanes from Saint Raphail. She disappeared in the Mediterranean and was never heard of again.

L.52, commanded by Oberleutnant Friemal, crossed the Lincolnshire coast near Mablethorpe about half-past seven and followed a more or less south-westerly course to Northampton. She then turned south and was next seen at Aylesbury. Passing on she dropped a big bomb which broke some glass at Kemsworth near Dunstable. Then on to Hertford, to the south of which thirteen bombs fell in fields. More were dropped fruitlessly at Hoddesdon and at Waltham marshes. At about half-past ten she was chased by an aeroplane which failed to reach her height. L.52 continued on her way and crossed the Thames by Canvey Island and went out to sea north of Dungeness soon after eleven o'clock. An hour later she crossed the French coast near Etaples and passed on to the west of Arras and

St. Quentin, over Nancy, and by half-past five had crossed the French lines east of St. Die and so into Alsace.

L.53, commanded by Kapitanleutnant Prolss, came in over the Norfolk coast at Blakeney at a quarter to seven and steered a wavy course to the Crouch at Foulness. She then crossed the estuary of the Thames and the north-eastern corner of Kent, going out to sea, before nine, at Deal. She had dropped various bombs but they did no harm. She reached the French coast near Calais, and was near Reims at midnight. She finally crossed into Germany near Luneville.

L.54, commanded by Kapitanleutnant Freiherr von Buttlar, merely skirted the coast of East Anglia. Her bombs were dropped to no purpose. Buttlar was pursued out to sea for twenty miles by Flight Lieutenant C. S. Nunn, but the attack failed. He got back by the usual North Sea route, the only one to do so. Buttlar thus performed an outstanding feat in airship navigation.

Last, the L.55, commanded by Oberleutnant Flemming. She came in over the Lincolnshire coast at Anderby at about half-past seven. She followed an irregular course to the south and appears to have passed by the western outskirts of London and eventually out to sea at Hastings. Her bombs were also dropped to little purpose. She crossed the French coast at the mouth of the Somme, about midnight, and passing over the

French lines near Laon eventually succeeded in reaching Germany, but was wrecked to destruction on landing.

Nine naval and sixty-five military machines in all went up to dispute the sovereignty of the airships, but if the aeroplanes could not rise to the heights of the Zeppelins the latter were prevented from coming down to more propitious depths, and with what results we have seen.   Our aviators had a share in the catastrophe, which, although indirect, was no less deadly than if it had been direct.   Unfortunately, Lieutenant H. P. Soloman of No. 33 Squadron, who had distinguished himself in pursuit of L.42 on 21st August, lost his life on this occasion.   His F.E.2B caught fire after taking off at Gainsborough and he was killed in the resulting crash.   If in future Zeppelins were to be brought down in flames as of old, better aeroplanes must and would be provided. As the floundering airships approached London, the guns and searchlights were forbidden to open up; indeed, owing to the thick ground mists and the great height of the Zeppelins the searchlights could not possibly have lit them up; the guns and lights would, however, have given the airship commanders means for finding their positions and would undoubtedly have drawn the bombs on to the city with serious consequences.   If the airship commanders did not assist us we certainly would not assist them. Thus this raid became known as the " silent raid."

In all, some thirteen and a half tons of bombs were dropped, the greatest figure, with the exception for that of the raid of 2nd September, 1916. Thirty-six people were killed and fifty-five were injured. This was the only serious result of the raid for us.

CHAPTER XV

THE END

THE German airship service was now in sorry state. Disaster was being piled upon disaster. Zeppelins were being struck down faster than they could be replaced. Soon nothing was to remain but an obituary of a mortally stricken service. Hunted in the air whether overland or oversea, and bombed in their sheds, the airships knew no rest and no respite. As if in protest against such violent treatment they began to destroy themselves. On many occasions airships perished by storm and explosion, sometimes singly, but frequently in quantity. Thus on the 28th December, 1916, while entering her shed at Tondern, the L.24 caught fire. The flames spread to the L.17 and both ships were consumed with their shed. On the same day and at the same station the Schutte Lanz S.L.12 was damaged on landing and had to be broken up. The very next day L.38 was wrecked in a storm at Seemuppen, near Russia, while engaged in the raiding business. On the 17th June, 1917, the day Watkins destroyed the L.48, L.40 met a violent end in a storm at Nordholz.

L.57, which had been specially built to carry ammunition and medical stores to the hard-pressed German
troops in East Africa, never got there. She perished
by fire on a trial flight on the 7th October, 1917.
Then came the loss of the L.44, L.45, L.49, L.50,
and L.55, as a sequel to the raid of the 19th of that
month. But worse was to follow.

On the 5th January, 1918, an airship caught fire
in its shed at Alhorn. Other sheds were soon
involved, and in all, four Zeppelins, the L.46, L.47,
L.51, and L.58 and a Schutte Lanz S.L.20, were
lost, and in addition four out of the five double sheds
in the station were razed to the ground. This bon-
fire can be said to mark the funereal pyre of the
German airship service. It lost all hope and such
raids as were attempted in the sequel were carried
out merely to make some use of the ships which
remained. True, eight new Zeppelins were completed in 1918, but the Germans now knew that the
end of the airship service had come. They desper-
ately tried to maintain the attacks whatever the
results. Choosing only misty and cloudy nights
and keeping to their greatest heights—now some
20,000 feet—some semblance of life was artificially
maintained.

If such hopeless efforts no longer dismayed the
English, the disappointment and disillusionment of
the German nation, in its airships, might be warded
off for the time being, or obscured by the enthusiasm
of the aeroplane assaults. So on the 12th March,

1918, one ship attacked Hull in haphazard fashion while two others appeared to be looking for the airship sheds at Howden. One was unable to find them and gave up the search, going away with her bombs unexpended; the other, when within range of the Howden guns, dropped her full load six miles away and made off. Two others never came overland at all. Ten aeroplanes sought the airships in vain.

The following night Hartlepool was attacked by a single ship. She made Northumberland, and after lying off the land for some time suddenly crossed the coast without being observed and drifted over the town. The first intimation of her presence was the dropping of her bombs. The night was fine and the raider was sighted and pursued, but the attacking aeroplanes could not get high enough to reach their prey.

Second Lieutenant E. C. Morris of No. 36 Squadron, piloting an F.E.2D, with Second Lieutenant R. D. Linford as observer, rose from Seaton Carew shortly before nine. Half an hour later they saw a Zeppelin over Hartlepool at about 20,000 feet. They were then some 5,000 feet below. Morris climbed to his extreme limit—17,300 feet. Then both pilot and observer fired at the airship, but without result. They pursued her out to sea for forty miles until they lost her in the mist. Sergeant A. J. Joyce, also of No. 36 Squadron, went up from Hylton in an F.E.2B. After an hour and a half's patrol he crashed at Pontop Pike and was killed.

Next, on the 12th April, 1918, five of the L.60's left the German sheds, under Strasser himself, in an attempt to demonstrate that their tails were still up. The chief objective of the squadron would appear to have been the Midland manufacturing towns, and if so two ships did fairly well. One, which entered at the Spurn reached Wigan, and another which entered by Cromer found Birmingham. Each of these vessels discharged about two and a half tons of bombs. Of the other three, one flew about the Humber but dropped her bombs harmlessly on the south side, and so when she passed by Hull she had nothing to throw. Another raided Lincoln, with little result; while the fifth flew about the Wash and dropped bombs which fell for the most part where they could do no harm. On the whole, visibility was so bad that, except near Birmingham, the searchlights were of little use and guns could only fire by sound. Our aeroplanes were unable to ascend in many cases and where they were able to do so their operations were very much hampered owing to the eluding tactics of the airships which were favoured by mist and cloud.

For an expenditure of nearly ten tons of bombs seven people were killed, twenty were injured, while damage was slight except in the Wigan district, where several cottages were wrecked or damaged. This was all but the last of the airship raids on England. One and only one more effort was to be made and for all intents and purposes the Zeppelin attacks on England were now brought to a close; but the English attacks on the Zeppelins were by no means to cease. The British navy had set itself the task of completely eliminating the Zeppelin for all and every purpose.

On the morning of the 10th May, 1918, it was ascertained that a Zeppelin was working off the Heligoland Bight. Soon after one o'clock in the afternoon a Large America seaplane, with Captain T. C. Pattinson and Captain A. H. Munday as pilots, left Killingholme to hunt her down. After a three and a half hours' flight the Zeppelin was sighted a mile away heading for Heligoland. The boat's crew immediately stood by the machine-guns, while Pattinson climbed to 6,000 feet and overtook the airship. The Zeppelin had, however, seen the boat. Increasing her height the airship endeavoured to get directly over to drop bombs on her aggressor. Rapid fire was opened by the boat at 500 yards' range, and, although all the bullets appeared to hit, the airship continued to climb and, when directly over the boat, dropped five or six bombs which fell harmlessly into the sea. The race for height continued and when the boat reached 11,000 feet, fire was again opened on the target some 1,500 feet higher up. The port airscrew of the Zeppelin was then seen to stop and a considerable quantity of smoke to emerge from the ship which was making for Holstein in crablike fashion and sinking rapidly. The boat was now within sixty miles of Heligoland and, as the port engine commenced to give trouble the pilot was compelled to turn for home.

The Zeppelin, L.62, went down in flames, but the closing act of the drama was not witnessed by those who brought about her destruction as they were busy looking to their own safety. The flying boat had been compelled to land at sea on account of a faulty oil pipe. On perceiving this, German destroyers, which had fired at the boat during her encounter with the Zeppelin, at once made for the apparently shipwrecked aviators. But they were frustrated. Despite a very heavy sea Sergeant H. R. Stubbington, the engineer, climbed on to the top of the offending engine, repaired the oil pipe, and within fifteen minutes the boat was again in the air on a safe homeward journey.

Meanwhile, also the British naval air service had made other advances. The pioneer work carried out on the *Vindex* and *Manxman* in 1916 had demonstrated the practicability of flying aeroplanes from ships, but the landing of these machines on the decks was a more difficult matter. Longer and faster vessels were found to be necessary for such operations, and accordingly H.M.S. *Furious*, which was nearing completion, in the spring of 1917, was appropriated for the purpose. She was fitted with a large flying-on

deck forward, and on to this Flight Commander
E. H. Dunning had successfully landed a Sopwith
" Pup " on the 2nd of August, 1917. There were
various objections, however, to alighting on a forward
deck, and so it was replaced by a more suitable
flying-on deck aft. When alterations were completed
H.M.S. *Furious* became, in the spring of 1918, the
flagship of the Admiral Commanding Aircraft of
the Grand Fleet. Soon the Germans were to know
the *Furious*. During the hours which preceded the
dawn of the 19th July, 1918, H.M.S. *Furious*,
accompanied by the First Light Cruiser Squadron
and destroyers, proceeded to a position about eighty
miles from Tondern, where it was planned that
aeroplanes should be flown off and then proceed
to attack the airship sheds. Just after three in the
morning, three Sopwith " Camels "—each carrying
two 50-lb. bombs—left the ship and formed up to
starboard. A few minutes later a second flight of
four machines took off and formed to port. The
seven machines then headed in formation for the
objective. The first three all appear to have made
direct hits upon the northernmost of the two large
double sheds. This was set on fire and gutted.
Two of the three pilots, however, lost their way
on their return flight and were eventually compelled
to land in Denmark. Of the second flight, one was
forced by engine failure to land in the sea before
reaching the target; another, after dropping his
bombs landed in Denmark, while a third was drowned.

o

The fourth and leader, Captain B. A. Smart, who had organised the flight, saw, on reaching Tondern, that one shed had been destroyed, so he attacked the other. His first bomb missed, but the second got home. He then dived to fifty feet full out, to dodge machine-gun and rifle-fire. With just enough petrol left he reached his mother ship and was salved. In spite of the heavy casualties in machines and pilots owing to the prevailing cloudy weather, the object was attained. Not only were the two sheds wrecked, but two Zeppelins, the L.54 and L.60, housed in them, were completely destroyed by fire.

The last German airship raid on Great Britain fell on the 5th August, 1918. The weather was by no means favourable; although the sea was smooth the sky was overcast and patches of mist hung over the coast. Inland it rained intermittently. On no previous occasion had the barometer been lower. This was an ill-omen and contributed in no small measure to the resulting disaster. The thin atmosphere prevented the airships reaching their only haven of refuge; they were unable to utilise the third dimension in their endeavours to escape from the attacking aeroplanes. Five ships had left their sheds ostensibly to harry the English Midlands as if in protest against the vast mounds of ammunition which were accumulating behind our lines in France, for the great and final offensive which was to end in the complete victory of the Allies. About eight in the evening three were sighted from the Leman Tail lightship. They were flying on parallel courses, but soon after deployed into V formation. The leading ship, L.70, had on board Fregatten-kapitan Strasser, the head of the German naval airship service. At about a quarter to ten she was just north of Cromer, with L.65 on her starboard quarter and L.53 on her port.

On receipt of warning of the approach of Zeppelins, nine machines had risen from the naval air station at Yarmouth. Major E. Cadbury in a D.H.4, with Captain R. Leckie as observer, left the aerodrome a few minutes after nine and made straight for Strasser's formation. Shortly after ten o'clock L.70 was abeam Cadbury's machine and some 2,000 feet above it. Cadbury was now at some 15,000 feet and quickly climbed to within striking range. He attacked the airship head on and slightly to port. Leckie fired into her bows; a great hole was blown in the fabric and a fire started which soon enveloped the whole airship. She raised her bows as if in an effort to escape and then plunged seaward—a blazing mass. Thus passed out the most powerful and most recent product of German airship ingenuity. Her seven engines combined to give 1,800 horse power; they could drive her at over seventy miles an hour and she could attain a height of nearly 22,000 feet. But this did not save her. The loss of such a ship alone was a crippling blow, but when at the same time perished Strasser, who had for so

many years been the life and soul of the naval airship service, it can readily be understood why German airships were never again raised against Great
Britain. Strasser found his grave in British waters
about eight miles north of Wells. On seeing the
fate of their companion, the two consorts immediately
turned about and fled. At about half-past ten, however, Cadbury was ready for the L.65. He closed
with her and attacked, bow on, as before. A fire
was seen to break out in the midship gondola, but
at the critical moment Leckie's gun jammed and he
could not clear it in the darkness. With this respite
the airship's crew were able to extinguish the flames,
and the L.65, delivered from Leckie's ammunition,
survived the war. But L.53 had no such luck; she
was to suffer a similar fate to that of the L.70 six
days later, as we shall see. Cadbury and Leckie
landed safely at Sedgeford aerodrome soon after
eleven.

Two other airships, the L.56 and L.63, approached
Yarmouth at about nine o'clock without being
observed. When near the land both turned to the
north and flew along the coast. Both were near the
scene of destruction of the L.70 and both saw her
go down in flames. One, the L.63, then hurried off
home all out. The other, the L.56, turned about
as though to get away from danger but at the same
time go through with the raid. Her commander
made for Lowestoft, but such bombs as he dropped
fell well out to sea. Owing to some acoustic trick

of the atmosphere that night the explosion of these bombs was heard as far as Sheffield, 120 miles away.

In all, thirty-three aeroplanes had risen to the attack. Owing to bad weather the inland machines were not able to see anything. Lieutenant F. A. Benitz of No. 33 Squadron, went up from Scampton in a Bristol Fighter at about half-past ten. Twenty minutes later he landed with engine trouble. This was rectified, and Benitz ascended again just after eleven. After a fruitless patrol of one and three-quarter hour's duration he came down to land at Atwick and crashed. He was killed, and his observer, Second Lieutenant H. L. Williams, was seriously injured. Two naval machines failed to return; one, a Sopwith "Camel" from Yarmouth, flown by Lieutenant G. F. Hodgson, and the other a D.H.9 from Burgh Castle, with Captain B. G. Jardine and Lieutenant E. R. Munday on board.

The final score against the Zeppelins fell to the offensive aeroplanes working with the navy. The most recent means at this time for conveying aircraft across the North Sea to within striking distance of enemy aircraft in their home waters, consisted of specially constructed lighters, each towed by a destroyer. Each lighter was provided with a short flying-off platform from which a fighting aeroplane could be launched into the air; the necessary airspeed to enable the machine to rise was obtained by the parent destroyer steaming full speed into the wind. The practicability of this scheme was demonstrated at Felixstowe at the end of July, 1918, when Lieutenant S. D. Culley successfully rose in a Sopwith "Camel" from a towed lighter. This was put to the test of action almost at once. On the 11th August, 1918, during an operation by the Harwich force off the Frisian coast, such a lighter complete with Culley and "Camel" accompanied the squadron. Just before half-past eight in the morning a Zeppelin, already reported by wireless from the Admiralty as being in the vicinity, was sighted to the north-east. The squadron was turned sixteen points together in order to entice the airship seawards. This manœuvre, combined with smoke screens, excited the Zeppelin commander's curiosity; so much so that he followed in the wake of the cruisers and did not observe the "Camel" rise from the rapidly moving lighter. Culley went up about a quarter to nine and quickly climbed to 19,000 feet, taking cover in the clouds and putting his machine between the sun and the Zeppelin, the better to remain undetected. An hour later the Harwich squadron saw a burst of flame in the sky, followed by a cloud of white smoke and débris which fell rapidly near the Borkum Riff lightship to the north of the Island of Ameland. Culley's job had been well done, and the L.53 had ceased to exist. Guided by smoke screens, Culley was eventually picked up some two hours later. When it is considered that only on one previous trial had Culley

Top.—A Sopwith " Camel " rising from the flying-off platform of a lighter.   To obtain the necessary airspeed to enable the machine to take-off, the lighter is towed by a destroyer steaming full speed into the wind.   It was by this means that Lieutenant S. D. Culley shot down a Zeppelin off the Borkum Riff lightship on the 11th August, 1918.

Bottom.—A close view of the lighter complete with flying-off platform and " Camel."

To face p. 200

taken off from a lighter, and that he made his attack in the open and single-handed, his success is an outstanding achievement second to none of the many glorious records of the Royal Air Force.

PART TWO
THE AEROPLANES

PART TWO

THE AEROPLANES

CHAPTER I

TRIAL EFFORTS

WHEN the war shall be but a faded memory, the Zeppelin will be long remembered, but the Gotha will be forgotten. The German airship was a symbol of terror, yet it fascinated the public; the Gotha made no such popular appeal. Nevertheless, so far as air raiding is concerned, the Gotha proved the more sinister and deadly weapon.

Although when the war broke out Germany was in a poor way with aeroplanes, she conceived mighty projects with her modest means. With the fall of the Belgian ports there was formed the Ostend Carrier Pigeon Squadron, composed of the best and most experienced pilots in the German air force. Its mission was to bomb England, but this hoped-for goal was found to be inaccessible on account of the great distance which separated the English coast from the nearest jumping off ground. To enable the squadron the more easily to shoot the moon it was housed and quartered in a railway train with steam up. Again on a bleak December morning a seaplane unit hurriedly organised at Wilhelmshaven arrived on the mole at Zebrugge, which had already been scarred by the British monitors. Like the Carrier Pigeon Squadron it was cooped in a train, so that men and machines could be moved inland to safety at a moment's notice. A little later, in the same month, a naval aeroplane unit was sent to Flanders and settled in the environs of Ostend.

It was these units, and more particularly the two naval, which first invaded and bombed England. In fact they carried out tip-and-run raids for over two years, but their efforts were not very disturbing. The best achievement of this tentative and barren period was that of Deck-Offizier Paul Brandt. Piloting Lieutenant Walther Ilges on an L.V.G. he left Mariakerke in the early morning of the 28th November, 1916, with the intention of bombing the Admiralty. A slight mist or fog hung over the city that morning. The weather otherwise was fair or fine with hardly a breath of wind. Suddenly, like a bolt from the blue, a series of bombs dropped between Harrods' stores and Victoria station. They fell on a baker's shop, a dairy, a private residence, some mews, and on the Victoria Palace music hall. The six bombs injured ten people. Otherwise they did little harm. After this performance Ilges left London in a south-easterly direction, and when well clear of the city he became anxious about his return, particularly when he found himself over an aerodrome from which he saw two machines rising. He imagined the alarm had been raised and that strenuous efforts would be made to cut off his retreat. In order to dodge the naval pilots at Westgate and Manston he slewed round to the south-west and when at Tunbridge Wells turned due south. Ultimately he passed out to sea by Hastings. He then steered a course for Abbeville, from which point he thought he would be able to fly over the Allied lines and reach Lille. By this means he considered he would be able to avoid the Dover and Dunkirk air patrols. But his engine failed at the mouth of the Somme. Realising that with diminished power he would be unable to rise sufficiently high to cross our lines undetected, he decided to limp along the French coast in the hope of making Belgium without further misadventure. He got as far as Boulogne, where his engine gave out completely and compelled him to land. He burned everything except a map of London which was found undamaged.

Thus passed London's first baptism of bomb practice by German aeroplanes. It was to suffer many worse attacks. A considerable amount of shot and shell was aimed at Ilges and many machines went up to look for his L.V.G., but his height over England and the haze preserved him from destruction.

Next in importance ranks the first night attack on London by aeroplane. About one o'clock in the morning of the 6th/7th May, 1917, the inhabitants of the north-eastern metropolis were aroused from their slumbers by the bursts of a battery of bombs which dropped from the sky in a straight line from Hackney to Holloway. The moon was at the full, but the nocturnal Albatros was not seen, although some claimed to have heard it. The first bomb fell on Hackney marshes; a second, which killed a man and seriously injured a woman, on some mansions; a third on a gravel path in Stoke Newington; a fourth, which burst a water main, in Highbury Fields; and a fifth which was a "dud" in Lower Holloway. Four aeroplanes rose, two naval from Manston and two military from Bekesbourne, but they searched the moonlit sky in vain. The raider probably came from the naval unit at Mariakerke which thus gained the double distinction of first bombing London by aeroplane by day and by night.

For the rest, the campaign up to the spring of 1917 can be briefly summarised. The raids of the last months of 1914, before any German airship visited our shores have already been narrated. The first of 1915 took place on the 21st February. A hostile visitor crossed the front at Clacton at about eight in the evening. He flew to Braintree and returned via Coggeshall, Colchester and Shingle Street. Braintree was presented with two incendiaries and Coggeshall and Colchester a high explosive apiece. They proved harmless. One incendiary is said to have been picked up by a soldier and thrown into the

Blackwater river. Two days later H.M.S. *Hearty*
reported seven German aeroplanes passing over the
Maplin lightship at 4 p.m. flying very high, but no
raid matured.

Next in the forenoon of the 26th February two
hostile aeroplanes made an abortive attack on H.M.S.
Gordoba hard by the Sunk lightship. The day after,
two half-drowned German aviators, who had spent
a rough night at sea, were landed at Lowestoft by the
tug *New Boy*. They had set out from Ostend the
previous morning with the *Gorodoba* assailants, but
their seaplane fell into the sea with engine trouble.

Shipping attracted the attention of many of these
early flyers. Four were seen making for the Downs
on the morinng of the 20th March. One dropped
six bombs near a coasting steamer, but failed to score
a hit.

At ten minutes before noon, on the 16th April, a
Taube monoplane crossed the English coast at
Kingsdown. It made for Herne Bay where it went
out to sea, but it came in again at the mouth of the
Swale; it next passed Harty ferry and soon was
flying directly over the anti-aircraft gun at Faversham
which fired off seven rounds. The Taube thereupon
rose rapidly and went west to Sittingbourne on
which it unloaded five bombs. Faversham was
again found on the return journey. Over a score
of rounds from the local gun were greeted by five
explosive bombs meant for the explosive works.
They fell on cultivated land to the south-east of the

town. It then passed out by Deal. Some dozen
machines from Eastchurch, Manston and Dover had
gone up but they failed to find the monoplane.

They were out again on the 23rd May. In the
morning an aeroplane practised ship strafing near
the Goodwin sands and another in the afternoon did
likewise near Dover, but no success attended these
efforts.

Nothing further occurred of any consequence for
five months, when, on the 13th September a seaplane came to Cliftonville and dropped ten bombs.
Six fell in streets and gardens and four on the fore-
shore. Two women were killed, and two men and
four women injured. The damage done was slight;
two cab-horses were killed. Abortive efforts took
place before and after this attack. On the 3rd July
a brace of aeroplanes was scared away from Felixstowe by destroyers leaving Harwich harbour and
on the 14th September a seaplane approached the
coast near Westgate but disappeared seawards without coming overland.

Dover was the main objective for 1916, and four
efforts were made in the first month of that year.
On the 9th January a hostile biplane appeared over
the breakwater but was turned back by gunfire.
Next, an hour after midnight of the 22nd a hostile
machine loosed off four bombs on the town, wrecking
the malthouse of a brewery and a hotel. Seven
casualties resulted—one man killed, two men, one
woman and three children injured. Twelve hours

later two seaplanes attacked the naval airship sheds at Capel, but the five bombs dropped failed of their purpose. Six machines went up to attack but the enemy escaped.

On the afternoon of the very next day, the 24th January, Capel air station was again flown over but no bombs were dropped. Four of our machines attacked the lonesome bird and one pilot got within 300 yards, but his gun jammed and the raider was lost in a cloud. Next on the afternoon of the 9th February two German seaplanes passed over the North Goodwin lightship. On reaching the English coast one turned towards Broadstairs while the other made for Ramsgate. Seven bombs fell on a girls' school at Broadstairs, as a result of which two women and a girl were injured. The Ramsgate raider threw no bombs on the town but aimed at a crowded tram-car on the Broadstairs road. He narrowly missed his target. His bomb did no damage. Their mission and their missiles discharged, the raiders made off to sea.

Eleven days later, on the 20th February, Lowestoft and Walmer were almost simultaneously attacked each by a couple of seaplanes. Lowestoft received nineteen bombs and Walmer six. There were two casualties—one fatal—and the damage was confined mainly to broken glass. Next, Cliftonville, was revisited by a seaplane on the 1st March. The seven bombs dropped, killed a baby and broke many windows. They came again to Dover and Deal on the 19th March, a Sunday, as well as to Ramsgate

P

and Margate. This time five were counted, but only three got back. One was brought down in flames over the Straits by Lieutenant R. Collis, who was flying in an F.E.2B from Folkestone to France at the time. Another, a Rumpler which had raided Ramsgate, was chased and brought down by Flight Commander R. J. Bone in a Nieuport seaplane from Westgate. It fell into the minefields off the Goodwins. In all, forty-eight bombs were dropped on the four places attacked. They inflicted many casualties. At Dover, where twenty-four bombs fell, seven persons were killed and eighteen were injured. Of the latter, eleven were soldiers housed in a hut. Ramsgate received fourteen bombs. Nine fell around the gasworks but did no damage. One fell on the driving seat of a motor-car, blowing the driver to pieces. The same bomb killed four children on their way to Sunday school and wounded nine others. The total casualties for the raid were fourteen killed and twenty-six injured. There was a certain amount of damage to property, but nothing considerable.

Dover was again reconnoitred by single machines on the 23rd and 24th April, and Deal revisited on the 3rd May, when nine bombs injured four and demolished a public house.

The monotonous catalogue continues, but meanwhile, it might be supposed that because these early raids merely affected the south-eastern coastal towns they excited little apprehension. This, however, was not the case.

A phenomenon peculiar to the air force was early observed at the front. Complaints would be made that hostile aeroplanes were coming over the lines unhindered. These complaints would generally be made simultaneously by both sides. The reason is not far to seek. Until aerial tactics were learnt by experience it was supposed by some that a defensive aerial barrage could be put up whereby hostile machines could be prevented from crossing the lines. Such attempts as were made on this theory proved disastrous to the defenders. The purely defensive flights absorbed an enormous number of machines which were thus not available for their work of reconnaissance and artillery spotting. Further, no defensive air formation, however numerous, could prevent a determined pilot from breaking through at some point. The far better policy was the relentless offensive against the hostile aircraft in which hostile machines were not only sought and engaged on their way to the front, but harassed also on their aerodromes. It is only when sufficient fighting machines were available for such duties that the surplus could be used to strengthen the defence. The best defence at the time was the one adopted, namely, a vigorous offensive at the enemy's aerial centre of gravity, and in this our pilots in France and Flanders were predominant and pre-eminent.

To resume. In the small hours of the 20th May, five machines attacked Dover, Deal and Broadstairs by moonlight. Fifty-nine bombs were dropped, but the damage done was surprisingly small. There were, however, some casualties; a soldier was killed, a seaman wounded, and a woman slightly injured. All did not return safely from the moonlight trip. At 7 a.m., Flight Sub-Lieutenant R. S. Dallas in a Nieuport Scout from Dunkirk, was four miles off Blankenberghe when in between clouds he caught a glimpse of a doubtful machine. On coming down to 6,000 feet, Dallas, in a clear space in the mist, observed it to be a German seaplane and dived on to it, firing half a tray as he closed. The German swerved, then dropped, and on being followed down was seen to roll over, sideslip and disappear under the surface of the sea. Dallas then proceeded to spray a German motor-boat in the vicinity with his unexpended ammunition.

There was a pause of some seven weeks before the next attempt, on the morning of the 9th July, when an enemy machine was sighted off the north coast of Kent. It had apparently come to reconnoitre the Manston aerodrome, for it threw no bombs. One of the machines which went up to attack, overhauled it forty miles out at sea and fired two trays of ammunition into it without apparent effect. The German returned the fire, likewise without effect. On the same day a second machine came to Dover at midnight and left behind seven bombs which fell harmlessly. Dover was again the objective on the 12th August and the 22nd September

A month later, on the 22nd of October, an aeroplane was heard over Sheerness. It dropped four bombs, of which three plunged into the harbour, while the fourth fell on to the dockyard railway station. The next day Margate was once again struck. Then followed Ilges' London effort which has already been described.

After a respectable respite the attacks were renewed on the 14th February, 1917, when a hostile aeroplane was seen over Deal at about eight in the morning. After that nothing further was seen or heard of it. This reminder was followed by another onslaught on Broadstairs on the 1st March, when nine bombs caused injuries to six persons. On the 16th of March 1917, an aeroplane came over and bombed Westgate, breaking some glass.

The following day a hostile machine came again to Dover. It dropped four bombs on the submarine enclosure without, however, doing any damage. A fifth, an incendiary, spent itself on a cliff.

Broadstairs and Ramsgate were again visited by a single raider on the 5th April, but nothing worth mentioning resulted.

So far the aeroplane and seaplane demonstrations were not distressing. True, conditions were rendered somewhat uncomfortable for the south-east coastal towns, but nothing had occurred to influence the war particularly or seriously disturb the morale of the British public. But the aeroplane raids next to come were different. They were definitely and deliberately planned to decide the issue of the war. The German aeroplane service had recovered from its serious disaster on the Somme. They had copied our methods and had preceded us with their new spring models. Whereas in the summer of 1916 it was " God strafe England, our artillery and our air force," or "Has anybody seen a German airman?" in the spring of 1917 the German air service not only felt able to cope with its work on the western front, but considered that it could afford the very best and newest machines available for the bombing of Britain. They thought they could win the war by peppering the metropolis with bombs, with what results we shall see.

CHAPTER II

THE GREAT DAYLIGHT RAIDS

ON the afternoon of the 25th May, 1917, the weather in Belgium was fairly clear and few clouds obscured the western horizon. Twenty-three most formidable bombing aeroplanes were straining at their chocks in the vicinity of Ghent on St. Denis Westrem and Gontrode aerodromes. They each had a full load of bombs aboard and were waiting for the "pistol shot." The objective was England—London if possible.

The machines were the new Gothas. Before the war many attempts had been made to build large or Giant aeroplanes. Sikorsky in Russia produced his "Russky Vitiaz" (the Russian Knight) in 1913 and flew it. This machine met with an untimely fate. One evening while Sikorsky was preparing his Giant for a flight a Gnome engine dropped from the air out of an aeroplane at a height of about 1,000 feet, and crashed clean through the Russky and wrecked it. The Bosch factory at Stuttgart thought about the problem but it was not until 1915 that the Gotha-Waggonfabrik constructed the first Gotha—Ost. Gothas first came into general use in the German air

217

force in February, 1917. They were large three-seater biplanes, some 38 feet long and of a wing span of some 72 feet. The power consisted of two 260-h.p. Mercedes engines, each of which drove a pusher airscrew. They were armed with three machine-guns, one of which was arranged to fire down a tunnel so as to ward off aviators attempting "to sit under the tail." They carried seven 50 kgm. (each about 1 cwt.) and six 12½ kgm. (each about 28 lbs.) bombs.

Such were the aeroplanes with which we were soon to become familiar, and such were the machines with which Germany calculated that the war would be brought to a victorious finish.

Those who attempt to work out the principles of war on mathematical lines deserve credit for their deductions. But as long as one has to deal not with natural philosophy but with human nature, formulæ will frequently prove fallacious in practice. Of this the Germans were being repeatedly reminded, but a nation which falls prey to easy sentiment is only discouraged when it is defeated, and even then it is not convinced of the falsity of its doctrines. If the Germans calculated that their bombs would strike such terror into the hearts of Britons that an insistent cry for peace would arise, they once again misread the national temper. True, the Gotha raids aroused indignation, but far from breeding panic, they only quickened defensive and retaliatory measures. The boomerang which the Germans had so confidently launched came back to spend itself in German air.

The Gotha

Used extensively for the German aeroplane raids on England

[To face p. 218]

Anyhow, here were the twenty-three Gothas. They belonged to the No. 3 Bombengeschwader or "Bogohl 3." This unit derived directly from the Ostend Carrier Pigeon Squadron, which was by now well trained and experienced for its task. Previous aeroplane raids on England had been carried out by the naval air service, but the Great *Angriffe* on England was allotted to military aviators. The start was ominous, for one machine fell at Thielt soon after taking off.

At 4.45 p.m. ten of the Gothas were sighted passing the Tongue lightship at a great height. They made their landfall in Essex, between the estuaries of the Crouch and the Blackwater a few minutes after five o'clock. They entered in groups, the last coming in ten minutes after the first. Owing to mist many did not see them. One observer at Burnham described them as "big white machines making a loud noise," while another who saw one said it was "silver colour, appeared like an aeroplane but made a noise like a Zeppelin." They all made for the Thames, which they reached in the neighbourhood of Gravesend. Then they swerved to the south-east away from London and gathered themselves into small formations, the better to defend themselves if attacked. The first bombs were dropped at 5.42 p.m., when 112-pounders fell at Luddesdown and Harvel, near Wrotham. They did no damage. One failed to explode but slightly injured an officer, who subsequently examined it.

After crossing the North Downs the hostile aircraft passed to the south of Maidstone where bombs were dropped at Linton and Marden. They killed a sheep. Further fruitless bombs were thrown until Ashford was reached. One, which fell here, burst forty feet in the air above a street. It killed a woman, and injured two men and a boy. Next they carried on to Lympne, bombing by the way as they went. The aerodrome came in for a shower, and many burst in the middle without, however, doing any damage. Hythe next received attention. A woman was killed; a man was mortally wounded, and a man and woman injured. Bombs which fell on the military camp at Shorncliffe killed sixteen Canadian soldiers and injured ninety others. Folkestone was then passed over and bombed; sixteen men, thirty women and twenty-five children were killed and ninety-two people were injured.

The Gothas now went out to sea fired at by the anti-aircraft guns at Capel and Dover but without result. They were pursued by machines of both services. Thirty-three of the Royal Flying Corps were unable to get into contact with the enemy; they could not reach the height of the raiders, variously estimated between 12,000 and 17,000 feet. A ferry pilot from Lympne, however, was able to get close up to one, but when at point blank range, his gun jammed and so the opportunity was lost. One of the naval pilots, Flight Lieutenant R. F. S. Leslie, who went up from Dover, succeeded in engaging a Gotha midway between Dover and Gravelines. He fought it at 12,000 feet and fired 150 rounds at about 100 yards' range. Tracers were seen to enter the fuselage and large quantities of black smoke came from the engine. Leslie was compelled to break off the fight owing to being mobbed by other Gothas. The Dunkirk pilots claimed two and the Germans admitted one "crashed in flames in the Channel owing to British anti-aircraft fire." In all, 159 bombs weighing some 3½ tons were dropped. The casualties were 95 killed and 192 injured, or a formidable grand total of 287 killed and injured.

The next attack was on the 5th June, when twenty-two Gothas assailed Sheerness, Shoeburyness and places in the vicinity. On this occasion fifty-one large and thirteen smaller bombs were counted, and the total casualties were thirteen killed and thirty-four injured. One raider, however, paid the penalty. He was brought down by the anti-aircraft guns. Gotha No. 660 came down at 6.31 p.m. in the sea 3,000 yards north of Barton's Point.

On the third occasion the Gothas headed straight for London and found the City. The morning of the 13th June, 1917, was brilliantly fine. The sky was slightly clouded, but hazy. Of the twenty-two machines which had been detailed for the attempt, two forced-landed at once with engine trouble. The score which got away came straight into the mouth of the Crouch except one, which had detached itself to make a sham attack on Margate. At Foulness three more sheered off, this time for Shoeburyness. The main body in diamond formation, headed by a leader, some twelve thousand feet up, kept on their course for the capital with the roar of their engines as an index of their purpose.

Having passed through the various gun barrages the Gothas reached London and dropped the first group of bombs between East Ham and the Royal Albert docks. The leader turned when over the centre of the city, firing a white flare as a signal for the rest to turn. The main attack was withheld until, at a given sign from the leader, 72 bombs were released within a radius of a mile from Liverpool Street station between 11.40 and 11.42 a.m. Three fell on the station itself. After dropping their main load the Gothas wheeled and seem to have lost their formation, one section circling to the north, and the other to the south. Six crossed the Thames above Tower bridge and dropped further bombs in Tooley street and in Bermondsey. The northward phalanx bombed Dalston and Saffron Hill. They then proceeded east and harassed Stepney, Limehouse and Poplar. 126 bombs in all, of a total weight of some four tons, were dropped on the metropolis, seventeen in the City of London.

Death and destruction were spread uniformly from Barking to Bermondsey, from Aldgate to Hoxton. The wreckage included schools, stables, sundry domestic works, a brewery and private houses, mainly in crowded quarters east and north-east. At Liverpool Street station one bomb which shot through the roof shattered a coach and ignited two others, while two fell on platforms.

The raiders passed out whence they had come. In vain did lonesome pilots hurl themselves against their solid ranks, and in vain did every available gun open fire upon the spent bombers.

Captain C. W. E. Cole-Hamilton, who with Captain C. H. C. Keevil as observer, had gone up in a Bristol Fighter from No. 35 Training Squadron at Northolt, attacked three enemy machines over Ilford. The Gothas returned his fire, and he only broke off the unequal combat after his gun jammed and Keevil was killed.

The five bombs dropped by the Margate raider injured a man, a woman and two children, while in Essex six bombs wounded a man and child at Shoeburyness. The casualties for London were, 162 killed and 432 injured, making a vast total for the raid of 594 killed and injured. These were far and above the greatest ever inflicted in any one raid. In fact, they were not far short of the total for all the Zeppelin raids of 1915, and with a tithe of the weight of the bombs dropped during these.

The sight of a formidable formation of enemy aeroplanes over London, swelled in imagination owing to the confusion between friend and foe, aroused the population to a passion of protest. They forcibly represented that such a thing should

have been made impossible. The full significance
of all this was not lost sight of by those charged with
our defences. The anti-Zeppelin organisation was
excellent, but neither the machines nor the measures
were suitable for attacking trained formations in
daylight. In short, the position was menacing.
As there were in England no trained fighting squadrons capable of meeting the raiders on favourable
terms, two were detached from the Expeditionary
Force to serve for a time on home defence. No. 66
Squadron was moved to Calais on the 20th June to
fly with its Sopwith " Pups " across the route of
the raiders and strike at them on their outward and
homeward journeys. Further, No. 56 Squadron
was sent with its S.E.5's to Bekesbourne three
days later. Whether, in consequence of these
measures or no, the next attack was not on London.
It took place on Harwich, the main objective being
the naval air station at Felixstowe. The Gothas
this time struck the coast at Shingle Street at seven
in the morning of the 4th July. They were first
encountered off the coast by Captain J. Palethorpe,
who was carrying out an endurance test of a D.H.4
aeroplane. He at once attacked the centre machine
with the result that the whole formation altered
course temporarily to the east. His observer, First
Air Mechanic J. O. Jessop, being shot through the
heart, Palethorpe was compelled to land.

The Royal Flying Corps' machines, sixty-six in
number, which rose from various places in Essex and

Kent and the neighbourhood of London, returned without having seen the enemy. No. 66 Squadron, owing to some error in liaison, went up too late. The weather became bad and they were compelled to return. The naval air service sent up seventeen machines in England and twenty from Dunkirk. The home machines failed to find the enemy. From Dunkirk a formation of five Sopwith " Pups " encountered the returning Gothas, estimated at sixteen, about thirty miles north-west of Ostend. The Sopwith formation proceeded to attack. Flight Commander A. M. Shook opened fire on the nearest enemy which fell, emitting clouds of black smoke. Flight Sub-Lieutenant S. E. Ellis dived into the middle of the hostile formation and fired over 300 rounds at one machine which went down in an erratic manner with smoke issuing from its back seat. All the Sopwiths returned safely to Dunkirk.

The casualties were seventeen men killed and thirty injured, mostly naval ratings at the naval air station at Felixstowe. The damage included a seaplane destroyed by fire, twenty-one pedigree sheep killed and twenty-nine injured at Trimley marshes, and broken glass. A rather interesting feature of this raid is the fact that of twenty-five machines which started from Belgium, seven were forced to give up owing to engine failure or bad take off.

The following day, Nos. 56 and 66 Squadrons were ordered to rejoin the Expeditionary Force. On the 7th July, the Gothas came once more to London.

There were again mishaps at the start. Twenty-four machines were to take part, but two were forced to land early with faulty oil pipes. Twenty-two were first located soon after nine in the morning well out to sea flying westward at about 10,000 feet. At least one went to Margate for a blind as had happened on a previous occasion.

The main body crossed the coast at Coate Outfall, near the mouth of the Crouch, in a diamond formation, reaching Burnham-on-Crouch ten minutes before ten. They passed through the gun barrage and made Brentwood, whence they turned off in a north-westerly direction in order to approach the capital from the north, probably in accordance with a pre-arranged plan to come over London with the wind, which observers in Belgium and on the German coast would assume to be north-west when in reality it was south-east. They approached London in two flights side by side with a common leader, thus giving the appearance of a single V-shaped formation. Each of these flights contained probably nine machines, and behind this again, at first close up but later considerably more in the rear, there was a small group of four machines. The squadron appears to have remained close together until met by gunfire, when the machines spread out considerably.

The attack on London was carried out from the north and north-west and thence direct to the City. Between 10.20 and 10.30 a.m. the right wing of the

Damage to the roof of the Central Telegraph Office (G.P.O.) as the result of a 112-pound bomb dropped by a German aeroplane on the occasion of the great daylight aeroplane raid on London on the 7th July, 1917. One man was killed and four others injured in the room below

To face p. 226

attacking squadron was reported as being seen from as far west as Hendon, Golders Green and Hampstead, whilst the left was over the valley of the Lea. They were flying in "terraced" formation as far as could be observed from the ground. Seventy-two bombs were dropped in the City and in the Metropolitan Police District; the total casualties were 57 killed and 193 injured. The number of bombs dropped was surprisingly small—an average of less than 3.5 per machine as compared with about double this number on the 13th June.

About a hundred machines rose to the attack. They came from naval stations, from home defence squadrons, from training units, from acceptance parks and from other places. It was an emergency force of very varied elements coming from all parts of the compass, but it lacked cohesion. The result was that while most gallant attacks were made by individual pilots the solid ranks of enemy aircraft remained unbroken inwards and outwards.

Second Lieutenant F. A. D. Grace of No. 50 Squadron, with Second Lieutenant G. Murray as observer, succeeded in bringing one down. They were sixteen thousand feet up in their Armstrong-Whitworth when they sighted the retreating enemy formation. When off Harwich and over the sea Grace caught up the rear machine and in the course of the ensuing fight he noticed a straggler flying below. He at once swooped on to it and Murray opened fire with useful effect as black smoke began to issue from the Gotha which was seen to fall into the sea. Grace and Murray fired several Very lights to draw attention to the wreck but were unable to remain in its neighbourhood themselves owing to shortage of petrol.

The naval pilots at Manston particularly distinguished themselves. One, Squadron Commander C. H. Butler, reported crashing a Gotha at sea twenty miles westward of Ostend. Another, Flight Sub-Lieutenant R. H. Daly, claimed to have brought one down in flames in the vicinity of Thornton Ridge, a shoal twenty miles W.N.W. of the mouth of the Scheldt, whilst Flight Sub-Lieutenant A. H. Lofft, who set out in company with Daly, reported that he drove one down off the Dutch island of Walcheren. In addition, Flight Lieutenant J. E. Scott claimed one thirty miles E.N.E. of the North Foreland. These successes, however, were not scored without loss. Second Lieutenant J. E. R. Young of No. 37 Squadron, who went up from Rochford on a Sopwith two-seater, was killed, while his gunner, Air Mechanic C. C. Taylor, was wounded; Second Lieutenant W. G. Salmon of No. 63 Training Squadron, who rose from Dartford in a Sopwith Scout, was killed, and Captain J. Palethorpe, who had risen in a D.H.4 from Martlesham Heath with Air Mechanic F. James as gunner, was wounded in the hip.

Once again a fighting squadron was brought home from France. This time it was No. 46, which came with its Sopwith "Pups" to Sutton's farm. They

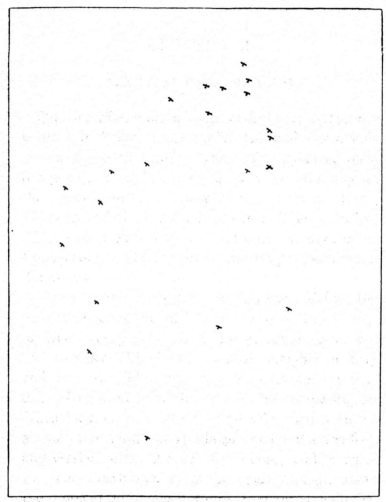

Formation of Gothas flying over Essex on the return journey after the great daylight raid on London on the 7th July, 1917. Of the 22 raiders one was not included in the photograph from which the above was reproduced.

To face p. 228

arrived on the 10th July but they never came into action at home, for never again did German aeroplanes come to London by day. Reorganised and rein-forced defences and the raising of three-day fighting squadrons had the desired effect.

The sixth daylight formation raid took place on the 22nd July, when Harwich once again was the objective. Sixteen Gothas came in shortly after eight in the morning at Hollesley Bay, but they showed no disposition to prolong their stay as they left twelve minutes later. Fifty-five bombs were dropped from Bawdsley to Harwich harbour with insignificant effect. The serious result of the raid were the casualties, mainly to service personnel. Thirteen were killed and twenty-six injured.

The home defence met with no success, but on re-ports being received that German machines were attacking England, a formation of Bristol Fighters of No. 48 Squadron in Belgium, went up to intercept them on their return. When about eight miles north-west of Ostend five Gothas were sighted at a low altitude. Captain R. Baker with Lieutenant G. R. Spencer as observer, dived from 16,000 to 3,000 feet on to one and shot it down to crash in the sea.

The last two daylight attacks took place in August, one on the 12th and the other on the 22nd. On the former occasion the number of starters had dropped to thirteen. Nine came over to Southend while a single Gotha made the usual Margate feint. The bombs fell mainly in the vicinity of Southend, causing thirty-two deaths and injuries to forty-six persons; the damage consisted of a few houses wrecked and some windows broken in residential parts. At Margate a woman was injured and an unoccupied house shattered.

One Gotha fell to the defenders. Flight Sub-Lieutenant H. S. Kerby, who had gone up from Walmer in a Sopwith " Pup," espied a Gotha about 4,000 feet below the main formation. Kerby dropped on to it and drove it down to the water, where he observed it turn over with one of the occupants hanging on its tail. Kerby threw him his lifebelt and then returned. He was unable to attract destroyers to the scene although he fired three Very lights. The Gotha sank and its occupants perished.

A big disaster befell the raiding squadron on the 18th August, when a raid in force was to take place. Twenty-eight Gothas appear to have started—fifteen from St. Denis Westrem and thirteen from Gontrode. When well out to sea, strong wind and rain compelled the leader to abandon the expedition. While they were attempting to return the wind increased still further and the squadron became scattered. Most of the machines were driven north over Holland where they dropped some bombs, and finally a remnant returned to Zeebrugge. Two were shot down by the Dutch in defence of their neutrality, and an unknown number were lost or crashed.

For the final day raid on England on the 22nd August, ten Gothas harassed the Kentish coast from Margate to Dover. The fifty bombs dropped on this occasion killed twelve persons, wounded twenty-five others and wrecked some houses and damaged a military hospital at Ramsgate. Five naval machines from Manston, three from East-church, six from Walmer and two from Dover were in the air awaiting the arrival of the hostile formation. They attacked the enemy with energy over Thanet, and afterwards pursued him down the coast to Dover, and at no time during his course along the Kent coast was the enemy free from constant and effective attack either from aeroplanes or guns. The accuracy of the anti-aircraft fire was amazing, two Gothas falling to the guns. A third fell to Flight Sub-Lieutenant J. Drake, who shot it down in a fight over Dover.

Home defence now being able to fend for itself, No. 46 Squadron returned to France at the end of August.

CHAPTER III

THE MOONLIGHT RAIDS

WITH the new measures for the aerial protection of Great Britain a complete reorganisation was effected, and means for combating the daylight raiders sprang up side by side with those in being for the Zeppelins. To guard the route to London three new fighting squadrons were raised, equipped and trained on the lines of those abroad. No. 61 at Rochford and No. 112 at Throwley held the Thames estuary while near London No. 44 at Hainault farm was ready to deal with hostile machines which evaded the wider net. For guns a barrier was projected with the intention of splitting up hostile formations some twenty-five miles from the capital, so as to enable the defending aeroplanes to attack them in driblets. Further, the anti-aircraft weapons and defences for the whole area within range of the German aeroplanes operating from the Belgian bases were placed under the control of a specially-appointed officer, whose command, designated the London Air Defence Area, comprised the south-eastern portion of England ranging from

Portsmouth to Harwich. The commander chosen was Major-General E. B. Ashmore, an artillery officer who had had a distinguished career with the Royal Flying Corps in France.

The defending aeroplanes were under the command of Brigadier-General T. C. R. Higgins, who was the first commanding officer of No. 39 Squadron. With the increased number of squadrons and the necessity for decentralisation the Home Defence Wing grew to a Brigade, being ultimately entitled the VI Brigade. But before the plans for preventing the daylight raiders were perfected they had already become obsolete.

According to German writers, the increased efficiency of our defences compelled the Gothas either to fly at enormous heights, certainly above 17,000 feet, or abandon the day raids. If raids on London were to continue it was represented that they would have to be done by night. Hence the daylight campaign ceased abruptly and another, far more difficult to deal with, was started. The moonlight aeroplane attacks marked a new era of rhythmic ruthlessness hitherto unknown and scarcely conceived. They were carried out very differently from the day raids and resembled rather the airship attacks. Groups of machines left the aerodrome, each machine taking off some five minutes after its predecessor. The scheme was for them either to reach the coast at the same time but at different landfalls, or to make the same landfall but at different times. This relay system made it most difficult for the defence, particularly as the target presented by even a Giant aeroplane was insignificant compared with that of an airship, and moreover, the aeroplanes were not filled with hydrogen gas.

So far as the aeroplane defence was concerned, there was only one thing to do and that was to shoot the raiding aeroplanes down in aerial combat. Fighting at night between aeroplanes was unknown and not hitherto considered practicable, but if the position was desperate it was one to which our pilots were accustomed, who before the night attacks had reached their full vigour had overcome all difficulties and once again found the remedy.

The German squadron which started raiding England by night was the same which had raided England by day. For their new adventure they were to be reinforced by a special Giant Flight (Riesenflugzeug 501). The giant machines were designed for transporting heavy loads of bombs and had from three to five engines apiece.

If we encountered difficulties in night fighting, the Germans met many in night flying. Pilots who were brilliant by day were blind by night. Their eyes could not adjust themselves to darkness and they lost their sense of equilibrium in the air. They thus suffered many trials and troubles before they were ready to bomb England by aeroplane at night.

The new campaign was opened by two machines which attacked Dover at about eleven o'clock on the night of the 2nd September, 1917. Fourteen bombs were dropped, two 200-pounders of trench mortar shell type, well known as " crashing Christophers." An officer was killed, six people were injured and some houses were damaged.

The following night, machines estimated as ten in all attacked Chatham, Margate and Sheerness. There was a most unfortunate disaster at Chatham. Two 112-pounders fell on the drill hall of the naval barracks where several hundred men were sleeping at the time. No less than 131 naval ratings were killed and ninety wounded. Six more casualties were suffered by Chatham, while Margate, St. Peters and Sheerness, although bombed, escaped without injury.

The sixteen pilots who went up from the defence squadrons saw nothing, but some had carried out a far-reaching experiment. The day fighters having no enemy to meet were chafing under enforced inactivity at night. So while the raid was in progress the commanding officer of No. 44 Squadron, Major G. Murlis Green, obtained permission to go up to try the possibilities of flying day fighting machines at night.

This was an untried course which was considered as involving great risk. The normal night flying machines were specially chosen for their stability, but single-seater fighters were much quicker on their controls and more easily overbalanced. The permission granted, Major Murlis Green, Captain

C. J. Q. Brand and Lieutenant C. C. Banks, all of No. 44 Squadron, went up to do or to die. They got up safely and patrolled for about forty minutes. Seeing nothing, they decided to return and face the most difficult task, the landing. They were all successful. The news quickly spread and in a few days all the day fighting pilots were flying their machines at night. By a singular coincidence a similar experiment was successfully carried out in France the same night and with the same machines— Le Rhone "Camels." These experiments were to have a very remarkable repercussion later on the Western front when aeroplane night raiding had long ceased to trouble England.

After these two successive approximations, increasing in force and distance penetrated, the Gothas approached on the third occasion, on the night of the 4th September, in full squadron strength, and some ten got to London while sixteen others made attacks above and below the mouth of the Thames. Bombs were dropped on Orfordness, in Essex, on London, on Margate and on Dover. In London bombs fell roughly on the circumference of a circle with the line Regents park—Barking as diameter. Of four aimed at Charing Cross station, one fell in Agar street, Strand, outside the main entrance to Charing Cross hospital, the second on the back of the Little Theatre, the third on Victoria Embankment Gardens, close to the Hotel Cecil, and the fourth close to Cleopatra's Needle. The base of the obelisk

The result of a 112-pound bomb dropped by a German aeroplane near Cleopatra's Needle, on the Thames Embankment, on the night of the 4th September, 1917. A passing tram-car was wrecked, three passengers being killed and three others injured. In addition six other people were injured by the same bomb

To face p. 236

was slightly chipped, but a tramcar that was passing at the time was wrecked.

Taking it all round, London came off lightly in the way of casualties, sixteen killed and fifty-six injured. The wreckage included the laundry of Islington workhouse, some stores and a few houses. The only other casualties occurred at Dover and Margate —three killed and fifteen injured for both places. At Dover two "crashing Christophers" fell on Priory Hill, but they failed to explode; one went through a house, the other fell in a garden, doing no damage.

It is known that at least one raider failed to return. The Germans stated that it crashed at sea. It may have been the machine on which the Borstal gun believed it had registered a hit somewhere between Cobham and Gravesend. Of the eighteen defenders who took the air, a few got into contact with the enemy, but the results were indecisive.

The difficulties of the defenders in dealing with the night raiders were so great that experts who looked into the problem were inclined to consider them insuperable, and at the time they were right. Night bombing was being carried out in France on a considerable scale by both ourselves and the Germans and as yet no adequate means had been devised to prevent it. Here once again the defenders of Britain proved superior to the prophets. If the gunners could not see the hostile aircraft and if the targets presented were too small to be picked up by search-lights, they did not despair. What the eye could not see the ear could detect. They had already made use of the binaural faculty for locating distant guns on the various fronts of the globe, and were not to be baffled by invisible but noisy foes at home. So they devised instruments for locating the raiders both as to direction and altitude, and soon learnt to distinguish the note of the friend from the noise of the foe. Curiously enough, blind men proved most efficient at this work.

From these aural observations the paths of the raiders were followed and plotted on squared maps which enabled the average speeds also to be found. By constant practice controlling officers were able to tell where an attack would take place within a minute. Anti-aircraft guns, searchlights and listening posts were arranged in groups in which all stations were connected up to a central headquarters. The groups in turn were in telephonic touch with the Horse Guards, the headquarters of the London Air Defence Area. When a raid started, all telephones were manned and the information which came to hand at any one station was rapidly passed to all other stations that might be concerned. Similarly, the flying squadrons were in touch with the Horse Guards and the batteries, searchlights and listening posts in their vicinity. At each squadron and at each group of ground stations there was an operations room in which all the telephone wires converged. There was also a large scale map of south-east England upon which was plotted the raid intelligence as it became available. The operations room at the Horse Guards was an elaborate affair. A number of operators sat round the table, each receiving news from a specific area. The information when plotted enabled the officer controlling the raid to envisage the whole position at any instant. If he saw a tendency for enemy aeroplanes to congregate in any particular locality he could quickly arrange for aircraft patrols to intercept them or for special barrage fire to be brought to bear on them. The whole scheme had been so carefully rehearsed that by the time the night attacks were renewed after a three weeks' interval, the raiders were very disagreeably surprised.

Of the twenty-one machines which we counted during the raid of the 24th September, only three got to London although nine made the attempt. The raid was somewhat similar to the previous one, except that Dover came in for a particularly vicious attack, no less than forty-eight bombs of various kinds being dropped there by some six machines. But Dover was not demolished. In fact, the damage done was surprisingly small and the casualties were only five killed and eleven injured.

During the course of the raid the whole area in the triangle, Mersea Island, London and Dungeness was covered with the routes of the raiders. London received thirty bombs which killed fourteen people and injured forty-nine others, mainly as the result of a 112-pounder which fell at the entrance to the Bedford Hotel in Southampton row. The front of the hotel was damaged and most of the houses and shops in the row had their windows blown out. For the whole raid the casualties were twenty-one killed and seventy injured. Of the thirty machines up none encountered the enemy. Two were claimed to have been brought down by the guns from Barton's Point to Port Victoria, but it is probable that each station claimed the same machine.

The raid the next night, the 25th September, resolved itself into an attack on the south-eastern districts of London on the part of three machines, and a series of attacks on east Kent between North Foreland and Folkestone, whilst a further machine made an attempt to enter the mouth of the Thames by way of the Essex coast. With the exception of the latter all the enemy machines crossed the coast of Kent between 7 and 7.30 p.m., and the country was clear of hostile aircraft an hour later. Of ten machines which took part, four made for London. Three succeeded in reaching the objective, while a fourth turned back in the neighbourhood of Blackheath, after dropping bombs which failed to explode. The casualties for the raid were not heavy, nine killed and twenty-three wounded, mainly in Camberwell and Bermondsey, where many dwelling-houses were struck.

Twenty defending aeroplanes had gone up and one pilot, Captain D. J. Bell of No. 78 Squadron, when between Joyce Green and the Thames, was fired at by an enemy machine at a height of over

9,000 feet and about 300 feet above him. Bell turned to pursue it and followed it east for ten to fifteen minutes, repeatedly firing at it. He eventually lost it near Gravesend. One Gotha failed to return. It had apparently been crippled or wrecked by the anti-aircraft guns.

After a two days' interval a series of four successive raids took place, commencing on the 28th September. The first was frustrated by thick clouds, and the raiders got no farther west than Hatfield in the north and Sevenoaks in the south. Although some twenty came, the majority left England without dropping bombs, while others unloaded over Essex and Kent. There were no casualties and the damage done was slight. The raiders, however, may have returned in reduced numbers. One was claimed to have been brought down by the Chatham gun defences, another by H.M. Monitor *Marshal Ney* off Ramsgate and a third by the Deal guns. Further, the cloudy weather may well have caused more than one to lose its way over the sea. The shroud which hung over the raided area prevented our pilots seeing anything of the enemy, although twenty were up groping and searching.

The next night four got through to the city and a further four got near. The rest were driven off or returned without facing the music. Two machines which approached Dover were prevented by the gun barrage from coming over the fortress, and one was brought down. It caught fire and fell in flames into the sea, leaving a heavy trail of smoke behind it.   Its consort thereupon made for home.   London suffered all the casualties but one and all the damage.   Fourteen people were killed and eighty-seven injured.   Of five bombs which were dropped between Kennington and Waterloo, two fell in the precincts of Waterloo station and caused considerable damage to the permanent way and rolling stock.   The damage otherwise was confined to dwelling houses, Notting Hill suffering most in this respect.   Four bombs dropped near Faversham were not so fruitful.   They fell in the mud close to the Uplees powder works to the north of the town.

Of the thirty defending aeroplanes which had risen, only one caught a glimpse of a raider and then only momentarily.   The enemy machines now appear to have increased their height, for they were estimated by our pilots to be about 14,000 feet up, some 4,000 feet above the bursts of the anti-aircraft shells.

In the third of the series on the 30th September, London, Chatham, Margate and Dover were mainly involved.   Eight machines reached the London district, while three or four others approached near but were driven off.   The chief feature was the deterrent effect of the Chatham guns which thwarted attackers approaching from Thanet.   Comparatively few bombs were dropped and the resulting casualties were not heavy.   In London three people were killed and thirty-one injured, while elsewhere eleven persons were killed and seven were injured, chiefly at Margate. Three bombs which fell on the Midland railway clearing sheds at West Ham damaged three locomotives, some sheds and some houses. Of the thirty-three machines up, a few saw something of the enemy. Captain W. H. Haynes of No. 44 Squadron in a Sopwith "Camel" engaged one over Lambourne at about 6,000 feet. Haynes fired 300 rounds at 100 yards' range and then lost sight of the enemy.

The last of the quartette took place on the night of the 1st October, when a few machines, out of some eighteen which came, succeeded in getting to London, although many attempted to do so between 8 and 10 p.m. Bombs were also dropped at various places in Kent, while a somewhat half-hearted attack was made on the Suffolk and Essex coasts in the vicinity of Landguard and Walton-on-the-Naze. One machine dropped a 112-pounder into Hyde park. The concussion killed all the fish in the Serpentine. The twenty-eight bombs dropped in London killed eleven people and injured forty-one, while the damage was mainly to houses. Elsewhere there were no casualties and practically no damage was done although forty-five bombs were expended, mainly on Kent.

Of the eighteen defending pilots up, only one saw anything of the enemy, but it quickly disappeared.

One effect of these persistent night raids was the rushing of people from the more threatened and crowded quarters to tubes and elsewhere for shelter.

R

On the night of the 24th September it was estimated that some 100,000 had sought refuge in tubes. The next night the number had increased to 120,000, while on the two successive nights, although no raids took place, people began to flock into the tubes in the early evening without waiting for any warning. On the very rumour of a raid thousands of people from the east and north-east of London left their homes and went to the tubes, where they proceeded to camp out until such time as the danger, real, prospective or imaginary, was over. They not only went there in entire families, diminutive girls or boys carrying the latest baby, but they took with them supplies or provisions, pillows and bedding on mail carts or otherwise, together with their cat or their dog, their parrot or their pet canary. They established themselves on the stairs, along the passages, or on the platforms, though in the latter case they aimed at keeping as near the door as possible—resisting all attempts on the part of the railway officials to distribute them better—their aim being to make sure that they would be among the first to leave again when the "All clear" message came. Should that message be long in coming they had still made all possible provision for spending the night in the tubes with such degree of comfort as they could expect. During one of the night raids it was estimated that 300,000 persons sought shelter in the tubes.[1]

1 *British Railways and the Great War*, Part V

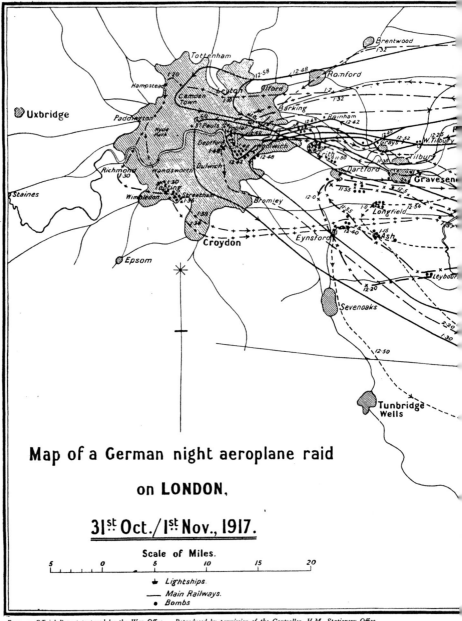

Map of a German night aeroplane raid

on LONDON,

31st Oct./1st Nov., 1917.

Scale of Miles.

⚓ *Lightships.*
—— *Main Railways.*
• *Bombs*

From an Official Report prepared by the War Office.   Reproduced by permission of the Controller, H.M. Stationery Office.

This map shows a typical night aeroplane raid on London. The aeroplanes would come over from Belgium in small groups on a relay system. The usual courses w
thus prolonging the raid over several hours.

In the particular raid illustrated, a continuous stream of enemy machines came in from the sea over Essex and Kent. They formed roughly six separate detachments
of London. Some twenty-four machines took part, about half of which attempted to reach the capital. Although none were brought down, many were dispersed by the

The German Air Raids on Great Britain, 1914–1918.   Captain Joseph Morris.   Sampson Low.

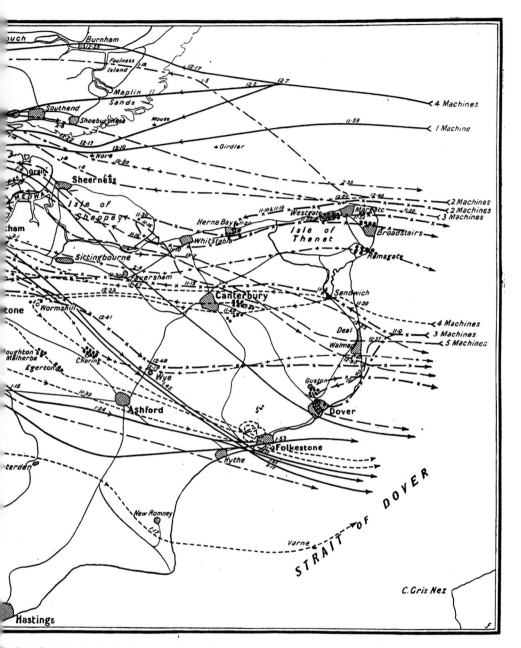

h and across Essex, well to the north of the Thames, or over Thanet and Sheppey. The duration of a raid varied. On some occasions machines would come over at great intervals,

each, with occasional single machines at intervals. Homeward flights were for the most part over Kent. The main attack was directed against the establishments in the south-eastern part bombs were dropped, but the damage done was relatively small. The casualties were ten people killed and twenty-two others injured.

Then again there was the interruption to works. Following a raid or even warning production was reduced and precision deteriorated.

The attacks were resumed on the 29th October, when enemy machines appeared at the mouths of the Crouch, Blackwater and Thames. However, the weather did not keep fine for them. They only penetrated a little and then went off. The few bombs dropped at odd places did no harm. Next, in the early evening of the 31st October, two appeared at Dover and bombed Langdon aerodrome and then went away. Later in the evening a continuous stream of machines came from the sea over Essex and Kent. They came up the Crouch and over Sheppey, Thanet and via Deal. There were twenty-four in all and about half attempted to reach London, but many were driven off or dispersed by the guns. Those that broke through the barrage attacked the docks and south-eastern riverside establishments. However, no very serious damage was done—a few houses were wrecked. The casualties were, ten people killed and twenty-two injured, mainly in London.

The defending machines were still unable to do anything decisive, but they were gaining experience and preparing themselves, and were soon to reap the reward. The difficulties were enormous. To the danger of being hit by gunfire was now added the danger of mistaking friends for foes. Of course, our machines had recognition signals, but on meeting another machine there was hardly time to make the signal and wait for the reply, because if the machine encountered was hostile it would have had time to disappear. Again, the pilots could not normally see a machine at night unless it was lit up by searchlights. Further, the flash from the machine-gun fire in action completely blinded pilots, and unless they were right on to their target they lost it, with little possibility of picking it up again.

CHAPTER IV

THE GIANT OFFENSIVE

WITH the improvement in the anti-aircraft defences of Britain the twin-engined night bombers of Germany found themselves in precarious straits. British guns were shooting them down and British aviators were becoming more and more persistent in their endeavours to force decisive combats. There remained for Germany one last hope—the Giants. These were to take over the main load of bombs, and sundry Gothas, flying light, were to act as escorts or deliver feints to divert the attention of the defenders away from the Giants. Among others, it was planned that the greater craft should carry a 300 kgm. bomb, that is, roughly, one weighing 6 cwts. Such bombs had already been carried by airships but not commonly by aeroplanes, certainly not by German aeroplanes raiding England. Another feature of the new scheme was to send over odd Giants at intervals with enormous loads of incendiary bombs to cause widespread conflagrations and prolong the raids for several hours with the object of producing the maximum moral effect on the

British public. It seemed to promise well for the Germans, but like all the preceding efforts it came to naught.

Some Giants might have been used at the end of September, but we first became definitely cognisant of them during the raids in December.

Unsuitable weather, the great wastage in night bombers and the slow deliveries of the Giants, all may have contributed their share to the postponement of the campaign. Whatever the causes, the night attacks were not renewed until the early hours of the 6th December, when some sixteen machines, including Giants, came over to burn down London and terrorize the surviving population. No less than 391 incendiary bombs were counted, as against 30 of the ordinary high explosive type, and they were all carefully conserved for London. The raid started at about two in the morning and continued for some four hours. Sheerness got the first blow between two and three in the morning, Dover, Whitstable and Margate the second and London the third, by three successive groups during the hours mentioned. Six machines reached London, while three others were turned away by the outer defences.

One machine which entered near Canvey Island was hit at once by gunfire, and turning back landed at Rochford. During the removal of some of its equipment it accidentally caught fire. Another, which was retiring from London where it had been hit by the guns, came down near Canterbury and was burnt by its crew before they gave themselves up. A third is believed to have been lost on its way home.

Considering the widespread dispersal of incendiary bombs the casualties for London were extraordinarily small—three killed and fifteen injured. The damage done was likewise small. Fires were started here and there but without any serious consequences. Elsewhere five people were killed and thirteen injured.

Next, an unexpected raid took place on the night of the 18th December—unexpected because never before had an attempt been made with so small a moon. However, the country was under snow at the time and this compensated the raiders for the smallness of the moon, as the course of the Thames could be distinctly seen from the air. Some twenty Gothas crossed the coast between 6 and 8 p.m. for the main attack, subsequent to which a lonesome Giant came over and succeeded in reaching and bombing London. A feature of this performance was the dropping of a bomb weighing 6 cwts., the first of such a calibre to be dropped over this country by hostile aeroplanes. It did not, however, accomplish much. It fell in Lyall street, by Eaton square, and slightly damaged twenty-two houses, but inflicted no casualties. On the whole, the casualties were not severe and the damage done was not great. In London thirteen persons were killed and eighty-one injured, while elsewhere one woman was killed and four people injured.

If, during the last few raids no mention has been made of the aviators, it is not because they were inactive. On the contrary, they were steadily increasing in efficiency and were soon to achieve the results of long and devoted practice. They had so far sought and engaged raiders with indecisive results, but on this occasion there is reasonable—if not conclusive—evidence that they scored their first success against the night raiders, and it is fitting that the experience should have fallen to Major Murlis Green. He caught up and engaged a raider between Goodmayes and London. Subsequently this machine, crippled beyond hope of return, fell into the sea off Folkestone and exploded while being towed in by a trawler.

The last raid of 1917 was carried out four days later, on the 22nd December, but not on London. At a quarter to six one machine passed over Westgate going west. It then turned and circled south-east of Margate and landed in a field near the Water Tower. It fired a red light before landing, presumably the signal for a forced descent. It was a Gotha, which owing to failing engines had dropped its bombs at sea. The pilot set fire to his machine and surrendered to the Margate Police with the other two members of the crew. Three hours later another machine passed over Broadstairs, turned over Ramsgate and went out to sea without dropping any bombs. A third was engaged soon after by the Thanet guns, and so it dropped its bombs at sea between Ramsgate and Sandwich and then went off. Such was the last raid of 1917.

The substitution of Giants for Gothas once more disconcerted the defenders. No sooner had the sound rangers become accustomed to locate the Gothas with reasonable accuracy, when a new and much louder noise appeared. The drone of the Giants was so considerable that on a still night their effect on the tympanum when twenty miles away, equalled that of a Gotha near at hand. Similarly, with the defending aeroplanes; they had reached a stage of proficiency in finding a Gotha, but when confronted with a mammoth machine, to which they were unaccustomed, they were confounded in their estimate of range. Fighting at night was a delicate, almost a scientific business, the slightest hitch or mistake and an opportunity was lost without hope of recovery.

Perhaps the calibre of our night fighting pilots is best illustrated by an example. One new to the business had just got on to an enemy night bomber in France and was about to open fire, when suddenly a trap door under the enemy observer's cockpit opened and a mass of silvery white objects enveloped his machine, whereupon an appalling fear of some new form of frightfulness paralysed him into inactivity, but only for an instant, for he straightway shot the enemy down in flames.

It was his first success and he did not mean to miss it. The silvery white objects turned out to be German propaganda pamphlets against the Americans.

The Giant campaign can be said to have been properly launched in 1918. The first attempt of the year was a failure. Three Giants with an unknown number of Gotha escorts had set out from Ghent on the night of the 25th January, but had to return on account of fog. Three nights later they came again. This time, accompanied by ten Gothas, they reached England, but an ugly misfortune befell one of the escorts. Captain G. H. Hackwill and Second Lieutenant C. C. Banks, both of No. 44 Squadron, were up from Hainault farm in their Sopwith "Camels," when they sighted a Gotha near east London. They drew up steadily, followed and fired at it until they brought it down in flames at Frund's farm, Wickford, in Essex. This was the first unqualified victory in aerial combat at night between aeroplanes, and if it was not so spectacular as Leefe Robinson's performance in first shooting down a "Zeppelin," its effect was equally far reaching. For the German night bombers it meant that their end was near and they knew it. During this raid there was an unfortunate disaster. A 112-pounder bomb fell on Messrs. Odham's printing works at Long Acre. Many people were on the premises at the time taking cover in the improvised shelter. The works collapsed and thirty-seven people were killed

The wreckage of Messrs. Odham's printing works in Long Acre as the result of a 112-pound bomb dropped by a German aeroplane on the night of the 28th January, 1918. Of people " taking cover " in the basement thirty-seven were killed and eighty-nine injured on collapse of the building   *To face p.* 252

and eighty-nine were injured. These formed about half the casualties for the whole raid.

An interesting feature of this raid was the fact that a hostile machine appears to have fouled the balloon apron in the Chingford district. These aprons consisted of steel cables suspended from a line held in the air by means of captive balloons. They were installed round the London barrier at some 8,000 feet up, in order to compel the raiders to keep above that height and so enable the defending machines the more easily to hunt them down.

The effect of the British aviators' success was reflected in the behaviour of the enemy the following night. Two machines, both Giants, reached London. One was viciously attacked by the fighting airmen who forced it to turn for home when near Tottenham, having hurriedly dropped its ton of bombs near Wanstead about midnight. They all fell within a distance of 300 yards, but there were no casualties and practically no damage. The other was attacked on its inward path at about 12,000 feet by Captain A. Dennis of No. 37 Squadron, who had gone up from Goldhanger in a B.E.12. None of Dennis' shots seemed to take effect, and the Giant retaliated by riddling the B.E.12 with bullets. It turned at Hertford and then made for Brentford. Its load of bombs was dropped on Richmond Old Deer park, on Brentford, on Kew Bridge road and in the Chiswick district. It then went home through

Kent, leaving the country at Hythe. A third Giant was defeated by the guns at Billericay and made off to drop its bombs elsewhere. On the whole the raid can be counted as a poor effort. Ten people were killed and as many injured. The damage was hardly noticeable.

Almost another month passed, when on the 16th February three Giants once more essayed London, but only one reached the objective. Its first bombs —five 112-pounders—were dropped on Woolwich. Then it persisted through the gun barrage and next dropped a 6-cwt. bomb which fell on the Royal Hospital at Chelsea. At Woolwich seven people were killed and two injured. The Chelsea bomb fell on a house at the east end of the hospital. It killed an officer of the Household Company, his wife, her sister and three children. Two other children were taken from the débris alive. The raider then made south-east and got rid of the rest of his load at Beckenham, where eight bombs fell harmlessly on some allotments and a park.

A second Giant apparently penetrated as far west as the Isle of Dogs where it was turned by heavy barrage fire. It dropped no bombs on land as far as we know. A third Giant merely bombed St. Margaret at Cliffe, near Dover, and flew out to sea again. Its eighteen bombs caused no casualties and only very slight damage. The next night only one Giant came and it got to London. The most serious harm it did was to drop five 112-pounders on the Midland Grand Hotel at St. Pancras station. These killed twenty persons and wounded twenty-two others. Most of the other bombs fell in the south-eastern quarter of London. In all, twenty-one people were killed and thirty-two injured.

Hostile machines were reported the next night, but there is a doubt as to whether any came over England; in any case no bombs were thrown.

A point which may appear of small moment but which proved of great importance, was the question of time. It was essential that all concerned in the defence of London should act in concert and simultaneously. In the aeroplane attacks seconds counted, and accordingly in January, 1918, Captain R. F. Wood-Smith, an officer on the staff of the London defences, principally concerned with searchlights, purchased a ship's chronometer and made arrangements at his own expense with Messrs. Dents to ensure that his chronometer was kept synchronised with that at Greenwich. Further, a search was made amongst the personnel manning the defences for men whose trades were connected with clocks and watches. One good watchmaker was found as well as a number used to the work. The good one was taught what was required and he in turn taught the others, and then they were distributed among the defences. By these means all the clocks were levelled. Even rates of error could now be measured and pendulums adjusted. So it came about that all clocks in the Defence Area were synchronised and no further mishaps occurred as the result of untimely action.

On the night of the 7th/8th March, 1918, six Giants set out from Ghent for an elephantine effort to break London. On the western front the Germans were getting ready for their great offensive—the final attempt to shatter the Allied armies in the field. To the Giants was allotted the task of undermining the morale of the British public and reducing their will and power to resist the German onslaught. In these Giants, the greatest heavier-than-air vessels ever flown, Germany concentrated her last eggs, confident that they would succeed despite the fact that all their predecessors had failed.

To add a touch of grandeur, a night was chosen when Aurora Borealis gives forth her streams of meteoric light with tremulous motion. In short, it was an exceptionally bright night, although there was a complete absence of moon. It was a most ingenious choice. If the raiders could not see too well, at any rate the defenders could hardly find them at all. The attack was carried out by five Giants, although it appears that six came; one failed to cross the coast. Three reached London; one went into Hertford and the last turned back at Billericay. On the whole, the onslaught turned out to be quite mild. London suffered all the casualties, twenty-three killed and thirty-nine wounded, but the damage done was relatively small. The worst disaster resulted from a 6-cwt. bomb which fell in Warrington crescent

Their Majesties the King and Queen viewing the damage done by a 6-cwt. bomb dropped by a German aeroplane in Warrington Crescent, Paddington, on the night of the 7th March, 1918. Twelve people were killed and twenty-three others were injured by this bomb, while no less than 400 houses were damaged *To face p. 256*

in Paddington. It killed twelve people and injured twenty-three others, and smashed up several houses, no less than 400 in the vicinity being slightly damaged, although only twenty were seriously affected. Three 112-pounders which fell at St. John's Wood killed eight people and wounded two others. Elsewhere, bombs fell for the most part harmlessly. The great Giant offensive had failed in face of the British anti-aircraft defences, notwithstanding the fact that the forty-two machines which had risen failed to see any trace of the Goliaths.

The German air campaign against Britain was now practically over, but the biggest air raid of the war was still to come. Following the failure of Germany's ground troops to end the war in the Spring of 1918, when the British army with their backs to the wall never shone more splendidly, the Germans started a bombing campaign on an unparalleled scale. Our bases in France and particularly that at Abbeville were signalled out for demolition, and for a time these raids were viewed with great apprehension. Simultaneously the greatest air raid of all time was planned and carried out on London, but like all the previous gigantic efforts it resulted in failure; and the failure in this particular raid was the greatest of all. Some forty machines were mustered for the event. Every available Gotha and every available Giant took part and London was visited by more hostile nocturnal bombers than ever before, but it was an unlucky number that reached the capital;

there were thirteen of them. It was a sadly defeated squadron, much reduced in numbers which reached home. Seven Gothas, perfectly good before the raid, remained in England, six reduced to ashes, while three more crashed on the home aerodrome.

Soon after ten o'clock on the night of the 19th May, 1918, a suspicious aeroplane appeared off the North Foreland and flew on a circular course from north to south. It then receded and dropped a flare. This apparent signal that the coast was clear was followed soon after by the arrival of the first raiders. The plan appears to have allowed each pilot a free hand as to the best means of reaching his objective. One Gotha kept a perfect course to London up the Thames. After unloading bombs near the Bricklayers' Arms station, off the Old Kent road, and Peckham, it was picked up at midnight, at Maidstone, on its way home by Major F. Sowrey of No. 143 Squadron. Sowrey, although fired at, got underneath and emptied two double drums into it which wounded the enemy pilot. By manœuvring it got away from Sowrey but was again picked up by Lieutenant E. E. Turner who, with Air Mechanic H. B. Barwise of No. 141 Squadron, was patrolling in a Bristol Fighter near Ash. They followed it east, shooting at close quarters notwithstanding the bullets emitted from the Gotha. Turner drew off with engine trouble but already the Gotha was mortally stricken. It came down near Harrietsham, apparently with the intention of landing on the aero-

drome there, for it fired distress signals. It crashed;
the pilot and one gunner were killed, while the third
occupant sustained a broken arm. The survivor
stated that when over London he had seen a big
fire. This was probably that at Messrs. Allen and
Hanbury's works at Bethnal Green, which had
received 4 cwt. of bombs. Next, one London raider
was brought down by gunfire off Foreness, near the
Elbow Buoy, just as it left England. It fell in flames
into the sea, but it does not seem to have sunk
immediately, as it fired one or two lights after striking the water. No wreckage was recovered.

A third which never reached London fell to Captain C. J. Q. Brand in a Sopwith "Camel" of No.
112 Squadron. He encountered the enemy near
Faversham and with his first shots put one of the
Gotha's engines out of action. Brand pursued it,
and a few moments later it burst into flames. Brand
was so close that his face was scorched. It fell
between Harty and Sheerness. Another which came
in near Wakering soon fell, for before it got a footing
it was hit by gunfire and dropped into the sea in
flames off the Maplin sands. One which came in
south of the Blackwater river landed with engine
trouble near Clacton. It made a bad landing, in
which the captain was killed, while the two other
ranks survived. A sixth which had reached London
was attacked first by Captain D. V. Armstrong in a
Sopwith "Camel" of No. 78 Squadron, and next by
Lieutenant A. J. Arkell and Air Mechanic Stagg in

s

a Bristol Fighter of No. 39 Squadron. They brought it down in flames over Roman road, East Ham. All the crew were killed; two jumped out from the blazing machine during its fall. Lastly, one was brought down in flames in the sea off Dover by the gun defences there and the wreckage was found soon after near the Knuckle light.

Considering the magnitude of the effort, the large number of machines employed, the fact that each Gotha carried nearly half a ton of bombs and each Giant half as much again, the casualties inflicted and the damage done were relatively small. In London 48 people were killed and 172 injured, while elsewhere only six casualties occurred, one fatal. A number of houses were wrecked or damaged, as were also a few commercial premises, but nothing commensurate with the eleven tons of explosives which were estimated as dropped on land. Thus passed the last and greatest nocturnal air raid on England and with it passed away the last shred of hope of Germany reducing Britain to impotence by air bombs. Only thrice again would German aeroplanes spy England, and then by solitary machines, which looked at Kent on the 17th June and the 18th and 20th July, 1918.

The high stage of efficiency which had been attained by our night fighting pilots is best illustrated, not so much by the decisive combats of the few, as by the uniformly good work of the many. How well this was done can be inferred from the fact that during the whole night campaign, from the beginning of September, 1917, to the end of May, 1918, only three pilots were killed and one observer wounded in all the thousands of flights carried out when raids were in progress. The fatal casualties were all due to crashes, and the single case of an observer being wounded occurred in action with a Giant on the night 28th/29th January, 1918. He was First Air Mechanic W. Merchant, who was flying with Second Lieutenant J. G. Goodyear in a Bristol Fighter of No. 39 Squadron. Second Lieutenant S. Armstrong of No. 37 Squadron was killed on the night of 18th February, 1918, and Captains A. B. Kynoch of No. 37 Squadron and H. C. Stroud of No. 61 Squadron on the night of the 7th March, 1918.

The rise and decline of the aeroplane campaign can be told by statistics. Up to the end of 1916 there were nineteen attacks in which bombs were dropped. The three tons of bombs expended killed twenty persons and wounded sixty-seven others. For 1917 there were twenty-seven attacks in which a total weight of fifty-one tons of bombs killed 655 people and injured 1,553 others, while during the last year of the war twenty-two tons of bombs were dropped in the course of six raids and the casualties were 182 killed and 430 injured.

GERMAN AIR RAIDS ON GREAT BRITAIN

PART ONE—AIRSHIPS

PART TWO—AEROPLANES

GERMAN AIR RAIDS ON GREAT BRITAIN

PART ONE—Airships

NOTE—All these attacks took place during the hours of darkness. Where the raids continued beyond midnight the double date is given.

DATE	LOCALITY	NO. OF BOMBS DROPPED	CASUALTIES KILLED	CASUALTIES INJ'RD	SEE PP.
1915. 19th/20th January	Norfolk, Snettisham, Kings Lynn, Yarmouth ...	25	4	16	17–19
14th April	Northumberland, Tyneside	31	—	2	21
15th/16th April	Essex, East Suffolk, Norfolk	78	—	1	21–23
29th/30th April	Suffolk, Ipswich	76	—	—	25
10th May	Southend	124 (120 incendiary)	1	2	25–26
17th May	Kent, Ramsgate	53	2	1	26–27
26th May	Southend	70 (47 incendiary, 23 grenades)	3	3	27–28
31st May/ 1st June	East London	119 (89 incendiary, 30 grenades)	7	35	30–32
4th/5th June	Kent, Essex, East Riding...	23	—	8	32–33
6th/7th June	East Riding, Hull, Grimsby	59	24	40	34–37

DATE	LOCALITY	NO. OF BOMBS DROPPED	CASUALTIES		SEE PP.
			KILLED	INJ'RD	
15th June	Northumberland, Tyneside	59	18	72	37–39
9th/10th August	Goole, Lowestoft, Dover, Eastchurch	83	17	21	43–48
12th/13th August	East Suffolk, Woodbridge, Essex, Parkstone ...	47	6	24	48–50
17th/18th August	Kent, Essex, London ...	107	10	48	51–53
7th/8th September	East Suffolk, London ...	97	18	38	54–55
8th/9th September	North Riding, Norfolk, London	152	26	94	55–58
11th/12th September	Essex, Epping	60 (52 incendiary)	—	—	59
12th/13th September	Essex, East Suffolk ...	27	—	—	59
13th/14th September	East Suffolk	46	—	—	59–60
13th/14th October	Norfolk, Suffolk, Home Counties, London ...	189	71	128	68–75
1916. 31st January/ 1st February	The Midlands	379	70	113	76–82
5th/6th March	East Riding, Hull, Lincolnshire, Leicestershire, Rutland, Kent	111	18	52	84–85
31st March/ 1st April	Lincolnshire, East Suffolk, Ipswich, Essex	223	48	64	85–88
1st/2nd April	County Durham, Sunderland, North Riding, Middlesbro'	34	22	130	88–89
2nd/3rd April	Essex, Waltham Abbey, East Suffolk, Northumberland, Scotland, Leith, Edinburgh	280	13	24	89–91
3rd/4th April	Norfolk	13	—	—	91

DATE	LOCALITY	NO. OF BOMBS DROPPED	CASUALTIES		SEE PP.
			KILLED	INJR'D	
5th/6th April	Yorkshire, Hull, County Durham	83	1	9	91
24th/25th April	Norfolk, Lincolnshire, Cambridgeshire, Suffolk ...	107	1	1	93–94
25th/26th April	East Suffolk, Essex, Romford, Kent	107	—	1	94–96
26th April	Kent	3	—	—	96
2nd/3rd May	Yorkshire, Northumberland, Scotland	129	9	30	97–101
29th July	East Riding, Lincolnshire, Norfolk	65	—	—	113
31st July/ 1st August	Kent, Ramsgate, Norfolk, Suffolk, Cambridgeshire, Isle of Ely, Lincolnshire	100	—	—	114
2nd/3rd August	Norfolk, East Suffolk, Kent	137	—	—	114–115
9th August	Norfolk, Yorkshire, Hull, County Durham, Northumberland, Scotland, Roxburghshire	186	10	16	115–116
23rd/24th August	East Suffolk	34	—	—	120
24th/25th August	East Suffolk, Essex, Kent, London ... ...:	102	9	40	120–122
2nd/3rd September	East Riding, Lincolnshire, Boston, Nottinghamshire, Norfolk, Isle of Ely, Cambridgeshire, Huntingdonshire, Suffolk, Essex, Hertfordshire, Bedfordshire, Kent, London ...	463	4	12	124–135
23rd/24th September	East Riding, Lincolnshire, Nottinghamshire, Nottingham, Norfolk, Suffolk, Essex, Surrey, Kent, London	368	40	130	136–142
25th/26th September	Lancashire, Bolton, Yorkshire, Sheffield, Derbyshire, Lincolnshire, Portsmouth	127	43	31	142–145

DATE	LOCALITY	NO. OF BOMBS DROPPED	CASUALTIES		SEE PP.
			KILLED	INJR'D	
1st/2nd October	Lincolnshire, Northampton-shire, Norfolk, Hertford-shire, Potters Bar ...	201	1	1	145–148
27th/28th November	County Durham, Yorkshire, Staffordshire, Stoke-on-Trent, Cheshire ...	206	4	37	151–156
1917. 17th February	Deal, Kingsdown	No bombs dropped on land.	—	—	161
16th/17th March	Kent, East Sussex ...	79	—	—	161–163
24th May	Norfolk, Suffolk, Essex ...	60	1	—	163–166
17th June	Kent, Ramsgate, East Suffolk	42	3	16	166–168
22nd August	East Riding	29	—	1	173–174
25th September	Lincolnshire, Yorkshire, Hull	97	—	3	174–177
19th/20th October	Midlands, Eastern Counties, London	273	36	55	178–188
1918. 12th March	East Riding, Hull ...	38	1	—	190–191
13th March	West Hartlepool	15	8	39	191–192
12th/13th April	Lincolnshire, Northampton-shire, Lancashire, Wigan, Warwickshire, Birming-ham, Norfolk	135	7	20	192–193
5th/6th August	Norfolk	No bombs dropped on land	—	—	196–199

PART TWO—Aeroplanes

NOTE—*Those attacks shown as taking place at night occurred between dusk and dawn. Where the raids continued beyond midnight the double dates are given.*

DATE	D = BY DAY N = BY NGT.	LOCALITY	NO. OF BOMBS DROPPED	CASUALTIES KILL'D	INJ'D	SEE PP.
1914. 24th December	D	Dover	1	—	—	16
25th December	D	Thames up to Erith	2 (On Cliffe, Kent)	—	—	16
1915. 21st February	N	Essex, Braintree, Cog-geshall, Colchester	4	—	—	208–209
16th April	D	Kent, Faversham, Sit-tingbourne, Deal	10	—	—	209–210
3rd July	D	East Suffolk ...	No bombs dropped on land	—	—	210
13th September	D	Margate	10	2	6	210
1916. 9th January	D	Dover	No bombs dropped	—	—	210
23rd January	N	Dover	9	1	6	210
23rd January	D	Dover, Folkestone...	5	—	—	210–211
24th January	D	Dover, Folkestone...	No bombs dropped	—	—	211
9th February	D	Broadstairs, Rams-gate	13	—	3	211
20th February	D	Walmer, Lowestoft	25	1	1	211

DATE	D ═ BY DAY N ═ BY NGT.	LOCALITY	NO. OF BOMBS DROPPED	CASUALTIES KILL'D	INJ'D	SEE PP.
1st March	N	Broadstairs, Margate	7	I	—	211
19th March	D	Dover, Deal, Margate, Ramsgate ...	48	14	26	211–212
23rd April	D	Dover	No bombs dropped	—	—	212
24th April	D	Dover	No bombs dropped	—	—	212
3rd May	D	Deal...	9	—	4	212
20th May	N	Kent, Dover ...	59	I	2	213–214
9th July	D	North Foreland ...	No bombs dropped	—	—	214
9th/10th July	N	Dover	7	—	—	214
12th August	D	Dover	4	—	7	214
22nd September	D	Dover	7	—	—	214
22nd October	D	Sheerness	4	—	—	214
23rd October	D	Margate	3	—	2	215
28th November	D	London	6	—	10	206–207
1917 14th February	D	Deal...	No bombs dropped	—	—	215
1st March	D	Broadstairs	9	—	6	215
16th March	N	Margate, Westgate...	21	—	—	215
17th March	D	Dover	5	—	—	215
5th April	N	Kent	8	—	—	215
6th/7th May	N	London	5	I	2	207–208
25th May	D	Kent, Folkestone ...	159	95	192	217–221
5th June	D	Essex, Kent ...	64	13	34	222

DATE	D = BY DAY N = BY NGT.	LOCALITY	NO. OF BOMBS DROPPED	CASUALTIES		SEE PP.
				KILL'D	INJ'D	
13th June	D	Kent, Margate, Essex, London	126	162	432	221–223
4th July	D	Harwich District ...	42	17	30	224–225
7th July	D	Margate, London ...	75	57	193	225–228
22nd July	D	Harwich District ...	55	13	26	229
12th August	D	Essex, Southend, Kent, Margate ...	37	32	46	229–230
22nd August	D	Kent, Margate, Ramsgate, Dover ...	50	12	25	230–231
2nd September	N	Dover	14	1	6	234–235
3rd/4th September	N	Kent, Chatham, Margate	46	132	96	235–236
4th/5th September	N	East Suffolk, Essex, Kent, Dover, Margate, London ...	90	19	71	236–237
24th September	N	Kent, Dover, East Suffolk, Essex, London	118	21	70	239–240
25th September	N	Kent, London ...	60	9	23	240–241
28th September	N	Kent, Essex, East Suffolk	45	—	—	241
29th/30th September	N	Kent, Essex, London	55	14	87	241–242
30th September	N	Kent, Margate, Dover, Rochester, Essex, Southend, London	92	14	38	242–243
1st October	N	Kent, Essex, London	73	11	41	243
29th October	N	Essex	8	—	—	245
31st October	N	Kent, Dover ...	16	—	—	245
31st October/ 1st November	N	Kent, Thanet, Essex, London	278	10	22	245

DATE	D = BY DAY N = BY NGT.	LOCALITY	NO. OF BOMBS DROPPED	CASUALTIES		SEE PP.
				KILL'D	INJ'D	
6th December	N	Kent, Thanet, Essex, London	421 (391 in-cendiary)	8	28	248–249
18th December	N	Kent, Thanet, Essex, London	142	14	85	249–250
22nd December	N	Westgate, Broadstairs, Ramsgate ...	No bombs dropped on land	—	—	250–251
1918. 28th/29th January	N	Kent, Margate, Rams-gate, Sheerness, Essex, London ...	62	67	166	252–253
29th/30th January	N	Kent, Essex, London	69	10	10	253–254
16th February	N	Kent, London ...	29	12	6	254
17th/18th February	N	London	16	21	32	254–255
7th/8th March	N	Essex, Bedfordshire Hertfordshire, Kent London	29	23	39	256–257
19th/20th May	N	Essex, Southend, Kent, Margate, Dover, Rochester, London	155	49	177	257–260
17th June	D	Kent Coast ...	No bombs dropped	—	—	260
18th July	D	Kent Coast ...	No bombs dropped	—	—	260
20th July	D	Kent Coast ...	No bombs dropped	—	—	260

GERMAN AIRSHIPS BROUGHT DOWN BY BRITISH FORCES

GERMAN AIRSHIPS BROUGHT DOWN BY BRITISH FORCES

DURING THE GREAT WAR 1914-1918

AIRSHIP	DATE OF DESTRUCTION	HOW DESTROYED	AGENCY — GUNS	AGENCY — AEROPLANES	PLACE OF DESCENT OR DESTRUCTION	REMARKS
	8.10.14	Bombed in shed		Sopwith Tabloid. Pilot: Flt. Lt. R. G. L. Marix, R.N.A.S.	Dusseldorf	Flight from Antwerp as base (See p. 9)
	21.11.14	Bombed in shed		Avros. Pilots: Sq. Cdr. E. F. Briggs, R.N.A.S. Flt. Cdr. J. T. Babington, R.N.A.S. Flt. Lt. S. V. Sippe, R.N.A.S.	Friedrich-shafen	Flight organised in England and operated from Belfort (See p. 9)
L.Z.37	7.6.15	Bombed in air		Morane. Pilot: Flt. Sub-Lt. R. A. J. Warneford, R.N.A.S. Dunkirk	Ghent	Destroyed in flames (See pp. 34-5)
L.Z.38	7.6.15	Bombed in shed		Henri Farmans. Pilots: Flt. Lt. J. P. Wilson, R.N.A.S. Flt. Sub-Lt. J. S. Mills, R.N.A.S. Dunkirk	Evere	(See p. 35)

T

AIRSHIP	DATE OF DESTRUCTION	HOW DESTROYED	AGENCY GUNS	AGENCY AEROPLANES	PLACE OF DESCENT OR DESTRUCTION	REMARKS
L.12	10.8.15	Gunfire	3" at Langdon Fort, Dover	Also attacked by several R.N.A.S. Dunkirk aeroplanes	Ostend	Came down at sea. Taken in tow by German destroyers Reached Ostend and wrecked (See pp. 46-7)
L.15	31.3.16	Gunfire	3" at Purfleet	Also attacked by B.E.2c. Pilot: 2nd Lt. A. de B. Brandon, H.D. Detachment, No. 19 Res. Squadron, R.F.C.	At sea off Kentish Knock	Airship sank. Crew rescued and taken prisoners (See pp. 86-7)
L.7.	4.5.16	Gunfire	6" H.M.S. Galatea		Heligoland Bight	Airship sank. Crew rescued and taken prisoners (See pp. 103-4)
S.L.11	3.9.16	Shot down in air by machine-gun fire from aeroplane		B.E.2c. Pilot: Lt. W. Leefe Robinson, No. 39 Squadron, R.F.C.	Cuffley	Destroyed in flames (See pp. 124-7)
L.32	24.9.16	Shot down in air by m/c gun fire from aeroplane		B.E.2c. Pilot: 2nd Lt. F. Sowrey, No. 39 Squadron, R.F.C.	Billericay	Destroyed in flames (See pp. 138-140)
L.33	24.9.16	Gunfire	London defences	Also attacked by B.E.2c. Pilot: 2nd Lt. A. de B. Brandon. No. 39 Sqdn., R.F.C.	Little Wigborough	Came down intact. Crew taken prisoners (See pp. 140-1)

AIRSHIP	DATE OF DESTRUCTION	HOW DESTROYED	GUNS	AGENCY — AEROPLANES	PLACE OF DESCENT OR DESTRUCTION	REMARKS
L.31	1.10.16	Shot down in air by m/c gun fire from aeroplane		B.E.2c. Pilot: 2nd Lt. W. Tempest, No. 39 Squadron, R.F.C.	Potter's Bar	Destroyed in flames (See pp. 146–8)
L.34	27.11.16	Shot down in air by m/c gun fire from aeroplane		B.E.2c. Pilot: 2nd Lt. I.V. Pyott, No. 36 Squadron, R.F.C.	In sea off Hartlepool	Destroyed in flames (See pp. 152–3)
L.21	28.11.16	Shot down in air by m/c gun fire from aeroplane		B.E.2c. Pilot: Flt. Sub.-Lt. E. L. Pulling, R.N.A.S. Yarmouth (Bacton)	In sea off Lowestoft	Destroyed in flames (See pp. 153–5)
L.22	14.5.17	Shot down in air by m/c gun fire from seaplane		Large America Flying boat H.12. Pilots: Flt. Lt. C. J. Galpin, R.N.A.S. Flt. Sub.-Lt. R. Leckie, R.N.A.S. Crew: C.P.O. V. Whatling, R.N.A.S. A/M. J. R. Laycock, R.N.A.S. Yarmouth	In sea off Terschelling	Destroyed in flames (See pp. 169–171)
L.43	14.6.17	Shot down in air by m/c gun fire from seaplane		Large America Flying boat, H.12. Pilots: Flt. Sub.-Lt. B. D. Hobbs, R.N.A.S. Flt. Sub.-Lt. R. F. L. Dickey, R.N.A.S. Crew: A/M H.M. Davis, R.N.A.S. A/M. A. W. Goody, R.N.A.S. Felixstowe	In sea off Vlieland	Destroyed in flames (See p. 171)

AIRSHIP	DATE OF DESTRUCTION	HOW DESTROYED	GUNS	AGENCY — AEROPLANES	PLACE OF DESCENT OR DESTRUCTION	REMARKS
L.48	17.6.17	Shot down in air by m/c gun fire from aeroplane		B.E.12. Pilot: 2nd Lt. L. P. Watkins, No. 37 Squadron, R.F.C.	Theberton	Destroyed in flames. 3 of crew rescued and taken prisoners (*See pp.* 166–8)
L.23	21.8.17	Shot down in air by m/c gun fire from aeroplane flown from H.M.S. *Yarmouth*		Sopwith Pup. Pilot: Flt. Sub-Lt. B. A. Smart, R.N.A.S. First Light Cruiser Squadron	In sea off Lodbjerg (Denmark)	Destroyed in flames (*See pp.* 171–3)
L.62	10.5.18	Shot down in air by m/c gun fire from seaplane		Large America Flying boat, F.2A. Pilots: Cpt. T. C. Pattinson, R.A.F. Cpt. A. H. Munday, R.A.F. Crew: Sergt. H. R. Stubbington, R.A.F., A/M. Johnson, R.A.F. Killingholme	In sea off Heligoland	Destroyed in flames (*See pp.* 193–4)
L.54 and L.60	19.7.18	Bombed in sheds by aeroplanes flown from H.M.S. *Furious*		Sopwith Camels. Pilots: (*1st Flt.*) Cpt. W. D. Jackson, R.A.F. Cpt. W. F. Dickson, R.A.F., Lt. N. E. Williams, R.A.F. (2nd *Flt.*) Cpt. B. A. Smart, R.A.F., Cpt. T. K. Thyne, R.A.F., Lt. S. Dawson, R.A.F., Lt. W. A. Yeulett, R.A.F. Grand Fleet	Tondern	(*See pp.* 194–6)

AIRSHIP	DATE OF DESTRUCTION	HOW DESTROYED	AGENCY		PLACE OF DESCENT OR DESTRUCTION	REMARKS
			GUNS	AEROPLANES		
L.70	5.8.18	Shot down in air by m/c gun fire from aeroplane		D.H.4. Pilot: Major E. Cadbury, R.A.F. Observer: Cpt. R. Leckie, R.A.F. Yarmouth	In sea off Wells	Destroyed in flames (*See pp.* 197–8)
L.53	11.8.18	Shot down in air by m/c gun fire from aeroplane flown from Lighter towed by Destroyer		Sopwith Camel. Pilot: Lt. S. D. Culley, R.A.F. Felixstowe	In sea off Ameland	Destroyed in flames (*See pp.* 199–201)

NOTE—In addition the following were lost, destroyed or surrendered, when returning from raids on England: L.19 (2.2.16); L.20 (3.5.16); L.39 (17.3.17); L.44, L.45, L.49, L.50 and L.55 (20.10.17).

GENERAL INDEX

INDEX